A Retirement Primer

A Retirement Primer
Asking and Answering the Right Questions

John N. Buxton

ORANGE *frazer* PRESS
Wilmington, Ohio

ISBN 978-1949248-050
Copyright©2019 John N. Buxton

Published for the author by:
Orange Frazer Press
P.O. Box 214
Wilmington, OH 45177
Telephone: 937.382.3196 for price
and shipping information.
Website: www.orangefrazer.com

Book and cover design: Kelly Schutte and Orange Frazer Press

Library of Congress Control Number: 2019938357

First Printing

Table of Contents

Prologue

A funny thing happened when I sat down to memorialize my thoughts and frustrations about our (Pam's and my) entry into retirement. First the words flowed out of my head as though this were the magnum opus I had been waiting my entire life to write. There was no stopping me. Paragraph after paragraph...page after page... and chapter after chapter just appeared on my computer screen, easily and fluidly. Chapter One—done. Chapter Two—complete. Chapter Three—really good, if I do say so myself. Chapter Four—in the computer; and then, bam...it all disappeared as seamlessly as it had appeared. In one not so memorable key stroke, or mis-stroke, my entire word document simply vanished into cyberspace. Had I hit page down? Did I slip it into a different document? Had my fumbling fingers hit X or A when I was meaning to hit S in combination with Ctrl? And after three tries with the best technology people I could find, I realized this was the perfect introduction to retirement. You have a loosely–constructed plan that seems foolproof until you realize you had not anticipated some obvious pitfalls and had forgotten Rule #1 for all planning: Begin with the end in mind, and once you know where you are going, sweat the small stuff.

When I approached our grandson for assistance in recovering those precious pearls of wisdom that I had creatively entitled

"Retirement 101," he wisely began by asking me some apparently obvious questions, at least obvious to him:

- ~ Did you save the document?
- ~ Where is it saved?
- ~ Did you back up your work?
- ~ Where did you keep the backup?
- ~ What is your computer's passcode or key to activate its Microsoft systems?

I have never been all that attentive to the details of versions of software, operating systems, or the mysteries of this black box with a keyboard; but I certainly was able to set up reports, produce documents, and access the information my computer had saved. You would have thought, however, that after 42 years as an educational administrator, I would have been technologically-literate enough not to dump three months of work in the blink of an eye.

I explained proudly that of course I had saved everything I had written by pressing Ctrl-S after every paragraph. Great, he said, where did you save it? What do you mean "where?" I saved it as a document. I realize that, he responded, but did you save it to the Desktop or to a special file? No, I saved it as a document…to which I got the "he really has no idea" look. Then he proceeded to do all in his power to bail his grandfather out—to no avail.

After two more tries with increasingly well-trained experts in the field, I was convinced my labors had been for naught. The 11,000 words were gone.

So how was I going to make the proverbial lemonade out of this lemon? Clearly, there was a lesson here or maybe a few important lessons; but before starting over, I needed to pout. Then I was back at the keyboard—sans notes or an outline—ready to try to recreate all I had lost.

First step: What did I learn from the teachable moment when I had lost all my work?

- ~ Planning matters.
- ~ Ask the important questions before launching.
- ~ Measure twice and cut once.
- ~ Consider the consequences of any action or inaction.

Coulda, Shoulda, Woulda.

If I had planned for retirement as I had entered the process of writing a primer on retirement, I would not have had the time to masquerade as an author because I would still be working for a living. Upon reflection, I am only mildly surprised that Pam and I are as happy in retirement as we are given how much we did not know and could have and probably should have planned for. We were not clueless, but we were guilty of assuming too much about too many things.

The purpose of this book is to work through the process that Pam and I went through on our way to retirement and, then, to share what we learned. This may appear to be mostly a book for and about couples, but as I hope to point out throughout this primer, it should be universally applicable. We did not have this framework available to us, so in spite of three decades of important training, there was so much we were not prepared to do. Furthermore, although we were coming into retirement with appropriate resources and knowledge, we believe that our experience is universally applicable, or at least we hope so. You do not have to have saved impressive amounts of money or have funds in off-shore accounts for this primer to be applicable to you.

First, let me explain the context of our move into life as retirees. One day I was talking to my parents about their decision to retire, then I blinked, and I was having the conversation with Pam about our timing and the upcoming date for our crossing over into retirement. How could it have arrived so soon?

Now, two things are important to understand: one that gave us obvious advantages and one that put us in a truly deficit position. First, I had spent 32 years as an administrator focusing on the compensation and benefits (and, yes, retirement benefits and funding) for a significant number of employees in large and complex educational institutions. I had worked closely with the Human Resources function as one school's CFO for 15 years, literally creating a modernized retirement program for employees. Compensation, benefits, insurances, and planning were under my purview; and while not an expert, I certainly knew a lot more than the average person about the puzzle pieces of retirement. Following that experience, I served as an administrator in another school for 17 years, and during that tenure I continued to have my hand in the total compensation questions that schools must work their way through as they attempt to ensure their employees will have an opportunity to be successful in retirement. I was perfectly positioned to know what one needed to do to be fully prepared for and secure in retirement.

However, the other side of the equation for Pam and me may not be applicable to everyone reading this book, but it helps to explain how and why we had come this far in life and not had to fend much for ourselves. We had been working in private schools our entire lives and the reality is that we would not be entering an assisted living environment; we would be leaving one. Anyone who has worked in a boarding school understands that many of the needs Maslow identified in his hierarchy—food and housing, employment security, property, safety, friends, and a supportive community (and, I would add, access to and funding for excellent education, and even retirement planning)—are made available in return for your commitment to serving the school as a triple threat—teacher, coach, and dormitory supervisor—in a 24/7 boarding school work model. You work hard and feel as though you are constantly on call, but you never receive the critical on the job training you need in order to have a realistic understanding of living in the real world or of living in retirement.

Pam and I were used to relying on the Human Resources Department to guide us in all ways on benefit matters. We had the incredible luxury of having fully-staffed programs for all matters technical (the IT Department), maintenance-related (Buildings and Grounds), and educational. We had huge and beautiful campuses to wander, hike, and enjoy; as well as nearly unlimited access to athletic fields and workout facilities. Nationally-recognized speakers lectured in our auditoriums, and the Arts Department provided wonderful programs of both student and professional performers. We had an exciting menu of events at our fingertips and never thought too much about how we would replicate all of this in retirement. Furthermore, we had never paid for housing costs; we had eaten with the students in the Dining Hall; and we had been assisted in so many ways by a talented and supportive staff. Now we were leaving this version of assisted living, and we slowly began to realize that we should have done more to prepare ourselves for the new realities of life outside the bubble. We had been subtly shielded from life on the outside and the obvious challenges of independent living.

So, with these countervailing winds buffeting us—knowledge unencumbered by experience—we set a date a few years out for our last year of work and went back to business as usual. We checked on our retirement funds periodically, made some assumptions about Social Security (based on not much more than hearsay, radio talk show hosts, AARP articles, political posturing, and television commercials) and agreed we would talk soon about where we wanted to live. (Remember, not surprisingly, that part of the accepted playbook for boarding school leaders is that they need to move away from campus upon retirement.) Regardless, deciding where to live really did not seem all that complicated, until we began to unpack that seemingly simple decision.

The first question we needed to answer was why we wanted to retire. In our case the sequence of the important questions was dictated partly by the fact that we worked as a team, so we were, in effect, having to answer the why and the who questions simultaneously. This will most likely not be the case for most couples; however, dealing with the why of retirement should lead logically to the second question of who. Pam and I would be retiring together, so we were ready to move on to the next key question: when.

The answer to when we would retire resolved our timing issue, so, quite sensibly, we needed to answer the follow-on question of where we would tell the movers to deliver our belongings. Those simple questions, while usually easier to ask than to answer, reminded us that life is always more rewarding if you start with the important questions. The answers to these important questions when one is readying oneself for retirement may not be obvious to all or even most people, but they are a good First Pillar in the process. We had begun with the why, who, and then the when question; and now were working on answering the where question. That left only the all-important what we would actually be doing in retirement.

I also recalled an apocryphal story about the author, Gertrude Stein, who on her death bed in a coma supposedly sat up dramatically and asked provocatively: "What is the answer?" and then collapsed and returned to her comatose condition. Those at her bedside were astonished. How is it possible that a person so close to death can have a moment of such lucidity? A few moments later, while they were still gasping in disbelief, she rose again to ask, "More importantly, what is the question?"

We all need reminding that asking the right question is a prerequisite to getting the right answer. A great leader once said that doing the job right is not as important as doing the right job. While this is definitely true in life and work, it is also extremely helpful advice for retirement. You would not want to have spent a life working toward retirement only to learn in retirement that you had been doing work, but it turned out to be the wrong work. Pam and I had lived almost five decades as educators. We had been disciplined and practical about so much in our lives—spending time with family, saving for the future, and separating what we needed from what we wanted. Retirement was never something we dwelled on. We were "look in the windshield, not the rear view mirror" kind of people, but we never wanted to forget to enjoy the present. We were pretty good at learning from the experiences of others, but we were clear that we had our own ideas and philosophy about how we would live our lives. We were determined that we did not want to be the playthings of fate and we did not like surprises, especially in important situations or matters. The surprises we experienced and those we avoided reminded us that if our experiences could be helpful to others, and if sharing them could serve others and help them avoid surprises, documenting our journey into retirement was worth doing.

A Retirement Primer

01

THE FIRST PILLAR OF RETIREMENT: THE FIVE Ws

---

*"If you don't know where you're going,
any path will take you there."*

One of the traditional markers for a leader is vision. Leaders need to be people with a vision for the future…for managing an operation…for leading a program or institution. Without vision, one may seem to be more of a daily manager of the process, taking care of the details but not attentive to the big picture. For years I believed that the requirement of vision may have been too daunting a criterion for leadership, causing some potentially successful leaders to disqualify themselves from consideration for the top post. Now in retrospect, I believe that leaders must have a sense of where they are going and what they want to achieve. If you do not know where you are going, how will you know when you have arrived at your destination? It is the leader's task (your task) to "put the picture on the puzzle box" and provide the vision of the future. That picture depicts both the goal and the destination. Answering the five questions, or at least grappling with them, is the perfect place to begin planning, and that's why it is the First Pillar of Retirement Planning.

The Why Question

While retirement may be an unavoidable reality, it can also be viewed as a destination. There are decisions that need to be made; planning that needs to be done; and choices that need to be executed in the service of that plan. All leaders understand that when you are planning to advance the process to attain the goal, you need "to set the plan and then work the plan." So, we all must begin, if we have the luxury of selecting our retirement dates, by answering the question, Why? This is the question that will provide the overarching vision for your retirement decision. You need a rationale for retiring. Otherwise, you may find yourself questioning the timing or even the reason that drove the decision. And this is not a simple matter. It needs to be a vision to which you are fully committed.

Our why was driven by our decision that we wanted to have the time and the freedom to spend more meaningful time with our family and with one another. Although Pam and I had been working together for nearly four decades, there were times in our life with our entire family—children and grandchildren—we were like the proverbial ships passing in the night. We have been happily married for 47 years, but we wanted to have the time to enjoy our last few decades without the inevitable choice of seeing and being with our children or working our careers. We wanted to be able to see our grandchildren grow and develop into the people they would become in real time, and not only on Skype or Face-Time.

That was our vision, and it was very personal to us. We certainly had competing priorities because we loved what we were doing in schools and we truly appreciated the fact that we were doing something important together. We loved going to work every day, and we had as fulfilling and comfortable an existence as anyone could imagine. But it could not provide us with more family time, so that was starting to make continuing to work a non-starter.

Every retiree who has the choice of when to retire (and it appears that the age for qualifying for Social Security benefits may be increasing as a way to extend the capacity of the Social Security fund to provide retirement security in the future) needs to have a good reason fueling the retirement decision. As we have said a number of times already, and as we will repeat throughout this primer, financial issues are important, but not the only ones that need to be considered. Medicare costs? The guidelines of the current Medicaid program? The costs of normal living, housing, and the plans for that glorious retirement? All these are financial in nature. But there are other reasons to pause and debate the retirement question. Retirement is not for everyone. There are those whose identities are tied up inextricably with their careers, and for them, simply retiring because of a date on the calendar or because of one's age, may not make sense. People need reasons to retire that are as well-founded as their rationale for staying in the workforce. Not everyone can replace a life defined by a comfortable routine, time with friends and colleagues in the workplace, or the experience of having exciting problem-solving experiences and supporting exciting agendas for a company or institution by replacing it with eighteen holes on the golf course of your choice. However, as we all know, some can. The why question may seem to be the most facile of the five questions, but as we will discuss later in the text, it may be the most important. A successful retirement is mostly about your readiness—personally, psychologically, and financially.

The Who Question

We no longer live in that 1950s, idyllic *Leave It To Beaver* world, and maybe we never really did. However, Pam and I grew up believing that was the world in the 1950s, and it provided certain possibilities and opportunities. In those days there was often a single breadwinner, and the non-working parent stayed at home awaiting the retirement of a spouse. At that time a person's company's defined benefit pension plan kicked in at the stated retirement age and was as regular and dependable as the milkman. The check was always in the mail. Furthermore, in those days your home, which was finally paid off by your retirement date, would be your retirement home forever, and probably represented your single largest retirement asset. Today there are many more options to consider. The who question is important because today many people can choose to work beyond the normal retirement age, if they want to or if they need to. Individuals have the decision to make for themselves, while some but certainly not all couples face the important choice of which one of them should retire first; or whether they should retire at the same time; and then, when?

Whether a couple is having this discussion for personal, financial, or health care reasons, the who decision is an important decision to get right. It may come down to one's inclination or one's capacity to continue to work, or it may be a decision for one person to begin working later in life that needs to be answered thoughtfully because there are numerous ramifications to consider. Imagine, for instance, that a married couple is faced with a situation where the primary breadwinner wants or needs to retire at the normal retirement age of 66, but the family still needs health coverage other than Medicare. That situation might prompt the spouse to seek a job with those much-needed health care benefits. Or, the wage earner retires and decides that he or she needs or wants part-time employment. There are many variables in this decision. (Note: This is certainly less of an issue for single people or for those without a living spouse. This is primarily a question for single income or dual income couples because it may be possible for the non-wage earner to decide to enter or reenter the workforce when the working spouse retires.)

Clearly, there is not one answer to the question of who. Many people have had their retirement dates circled on their calendars for years and are working toward that time feverishly. Others were all set to retire at a date certain until the unexpected happened—a change in family status or health. Regardless, families need to assess all options and have serious conversations about the possibilities and realities of each scenario.

Couples or singles can still retire and settle in for the Golden Years as members of the greatest generation did, or, as couples, they can address the challenge of who will retire as a serious question that has to be unpacked fully. One can decide or finally admit that it is not in his or her DNA to retire at all and then figure out how to make that approach work. You can decide that either you or your spouse will continue to work in order to preserve certain benefits that you cannot afford to lose for a variety of reasons.

Just understand that if you float carelessly into this next phase of life, you may be surprised…and surprises in retirement, as in life, are not always positive. Also, remember there are some decisions that you can undo if they prove to be unsupportive of the outcomes you were seeking. There are others, however, that are more challenging to roll back; so, think through these choices carefully. For Pam and me the who question was easily answered, probably because we were working as a couple, and when we had answered the why question, we realized this was what was right for both of us. Also, I would be retiring at age 70 and Pam would be 69. For reasons I will address later, working beyond this age would have delayed our reason for retiring beyond what was reasonable and, furthermore, it would have limited our flexibility with our benefit programs.

The When Question

The when question will complete the initial discussion about timing. You should have a good start at least on the questions of why you want to retire, or need to, and who should or will retire. Now you need to be clear about the when. Remember that all decisions should complement the over-riding vision or the why of your retirement planning.

Retirement has a variety of realities that every soon to be retired person should take into account. There are financial realities, to be sure, such as "Do I have enough money to retire?" These are accompanied by questions of health care in retirement and the psychology of no longer being in the workforce. Furthermore, and regardless of one's personal readiness for retirement, there are also substantial differences in Social Security pay outs depending on an individual's work history and actual retirement age. If one spouse were to retire first and the other spouse were to keep working, would that approach help address health insurance questions, Social Security decisions, and psychological well-being? That's why looking carefully and seriously at these questions makes sense. These are the right questions to ask, and they are not decisions to be made emotionally or by rote or default. Remember, the Federal Government made it unlawful decades ago to discriminate on the basis of age and, therefore, eliminated the required retirement age, so people now have a choice about when they will cease working and when their retirement benefits will begin. This is an important right of every worker in the system, so treat it as such.

If you are participating in a job-related retirement plan, there are rules and guidelines about when you can retire with some benefits and when you are fully vested, i.e. the money and full benefits are officially yours, without strings. You need to have read the fine print on your retirement plan contract, and if your workplace has a Human Resources function/department, check your understanding with that office. Often, the early requirement age is 55 for an employer-sponsored plan, but it may vary from 55 to 62. You need to know the answer to this question before you begin your planning, especially if you are thinking about retiring earlier than the normal retirement age set by the Government. There may also be other considerations, so you will need to determine what applies in your case. If you retire early, before 65 or 66, you will need to understand what that decision will mean for benefits that you expect to receive and whether you will you need to replace them.

In all honesty, Pam and I had somewhat naively planned an early retirement when we first considered the topic as younger members of the workforce. We believed that since we had been in a 24/7 lifestyle as boarding school people, an earlier than usual retirement age made sense. Sixty sounded good and would have meant that we had spent almost 40 years in a wonderful profession. As we approached that age and time, however, we realized we had more work to do and, in the interim, we had figured out how to balance our life and work needs satisfactorily. These were some of many factors that went into our when decision, and now nearly two years into retirement, we are confident that we made the best decisions for us about why, who, and when. Now we had to contemplate the last pairing of the Five Ws, the where and the what.

As you can imagine, these last two questions could arguably confirm for you your answers to the three earlier ones. However, I have scheduled them last in the lineup because I believe the hardest part of the retirement process is making sure you know the answers to why one wants to retire, who will retire, and when you will or should retire. Once you are clear about the first three variables, you can get serious about where you want to reside in retirement and what you want to do. These last two pieces of the puzzle are inextricably connected and will allow, actually even force you, to reconsider all the premises that led you to your answers for the first three Ws. So, answering the where and what questions will prove to be a great exercise in summation.

The Where Question

Now, for a couple like Pam and me coming out of 47 years of school housing and having never owned or even rented or leased a home, we had a serious question to confront. We could not stay where we were because we had the challenge of our children and grandchildren living 1,000 miles apart in two very different areas of the country. Fortunately, both were on the East Coast, so that answered the question of which part of the country we'd be looking at. And we had already determined in answering the why question that after being in a twelve-month-a-year career, we needed easier and more access to our families. So where on the East Coast was it going to be?

This deliberation could have been more difficult if we had already owned a home close to where we worked or had purchased a vacation or summer home back East. Now, some or even many people reading this may assume that if you do not own a second home or property, this primer is not written for you. In the boarding school world from which we were coming, it was normal for families to buy a home since they did not own what they were living in during the school year. Housing was a condition of employment for them; so, their "second home" was actually a primary home. But, even if we had had a cabin on a lake somewhere that we could enlarge into a true retirement home, the choices might have been daunting, given our children's very separate locations. But we did not, so our priorities remained clear. Family trumped all else.

Not so fast. What if we chose one of our children's two cities for retirement and unexpectedly a career opportunity took that family to a different location? We needed to look more deeply into the benefits of each location. We wanted to be near our families, but there had to be other factors for us to consider and put into the equation:

- ~ We loved being in the out-of-doors.
- ~ We loved the mountains.
- ~ We loved the ocean and large lakes.
- ~ We would be happier if we were near to our extended families and friends as well.

On all of this we agreed. We also understood we wanted easy access to international airports and to excellent health care facilities and hospitals. Check, check, and check...both cities in which our children lived met all these criteria. So, what would help us delve more creatively into the decision?

Both states had beautiful mountain ranges, easy access as well as proximity to the Atlantic Ocean and lakes, and a culture of embracing the out-of-doors. However, in one of the states the mountains were nearly a four-hour drive from our son's home and in the other, the distance to our daughter's home was only half as far. Then there was that fact that while both had moderate weather for much of the year, one had true heat in the summer and very little snowfall in the winter. The other had far milder summers and plentiful snowfall during the winter months. Yes, snowfall. Pam and I are both dyed in the wool New Englanders who happen to love snow and snow activities, even shoveling! We were beginning to see a pathway (no pun intended) through this problem.

Our next criterion was affordability. The real estate costs were comparable in the two states, but the tax situation represented a significant point of difference. This variable led us to an investigation into the differences in the tax philosophies and realities in the two destinations: Sales Tax rates? Property Tax rates? State Tax rates? Estate Tax rates? Taxes on interest and dividends? Also, we needed to understand general cost of living differences in the two states. All these things are relevant. These were easily identified. Less obvious, however, were the questions we were not sophisticated or educated enough to ask. Were there differences in the availability of insurance for Medicare plans in the two states? There were, but we did not understand what we should have known about this important part of the retirement process. Much more on this later in the Medicare chapter, but suffice it to say this was simply another level of differentiation we needed to understand.

My point here is that there were obvious questions that needed to be answered and then there were the not-so-obvious ones that proved to be equally important. This was clearly an error of omission on our part. You cannot know what you don't know, but there are things you need to know in order to make a completely informed decision. I am reminded painfully of those four chapters of my first attempt at writing Retirement 101 that I erased in a key stroke because I thought I knew all I needed to be successful. If deciding where to live is location, location, location; then preparing for a successful retirement is planning, planning, planning.

Lest you think this is all there is to understand, consider a few other issues related to where one decides to live in retirement. The once platonic ideal of settling down in a bucolic college town and enjoying all the benefits of the college setting may not be all it's cracked up to be. Many retirees may have seen the warnings about the myths of college town living for retirees that have recently been published in popular retirement magazines. Yes, college communities are filled with young people, but that means the emphasis on activities is often slanted toward the young. Not all college towns have as sophisticated medical facilities as larger cities. One pass through the internet about the facts and fictions of college town living for retirees should at least prompt the right questions. That said, we have friends living in college communities in the Midwest, and they could not be happier. There are very few one-size-fits-all decisions or plans.

There are also real questions relating to staying where you are or moving. What may at first seem like the most obvious answers to your questions about where to live in retirement may be worth some further thought. In our case whether to move or not was not even a consideration; it was a non-issue. Still, for most retirees there should be healthy, internal debate about the benefits of renting or leasing rather than owning and determining whether you keep your home or not. This might be an estate planning issue, a matter of ease of use and commitment of time, or a function of the cost of maintenance. Remember that for most people of retirement age today, their most valuable, single possession may still be their home, especially if it has no mortgage on it. And if it carries a sizeable mortgage, it may be the most costly and regular, financial commitment you have as a retirement cost. Clearly, some people have a hard decision to make, whether to "love it or list it"—especially once you have done the analysis of either retaining your home or selling it and using the proceeds to rent less expensively and to fund the what of retirement.

(Note: Some research I conducted suggested that considering a variety of factors when deciding which child in a family the retiring parents choose to live nearest to should include how much support—financial, baby-sitting, personal attention—will be required of them. The point being that moving toward family can have both benefits and challenges that need to be considered realistically.)

The What Question

In our case the what was clear and had been for a long time, but we were still in the process of answering the specific questions regarding what we wanted to do as retirees. We needed to be sure we had matched up our needs, wants, and wishes appropriately given our answers to and research done in answering the other questions.

So, we made a list of answers to the what question:

- ~ Family
- ~ Proximity to mountains and ocean
- ~ Relatively rural setting/privacy
- ~ Access to large airport and good hospitals
- ~ Some travel
- ~ Legacy planning

We had created our vision and the destination we had described as the "picture on the front of the puzzle box" we hoped to realize in our retirement. We wanted to make a difference as parents and grandparents for our children and grandchildren. We wanted to be able to engage in our hobbies of hiking and biking close to home to support our own well-being. We were clear that travel, while enjoyable, would be a minor commitment, but something we would enjoy if the timing were right. Furthermore, we wanted to make a difference both in the lives of those in our new community through our volunteer efforts and to those in organizations and activities that we believe in and support as charities. Lastly, we wanted to have additional resources at the last to support our children in their philanthropic interests and in their ability to make decisions about their grandchildren's education.

The answers to the what of our retirement planning have remained spot on and have not changed at all from where we were as we began both the initial questioning process and then the deeper analysis process. We have never wavered much from these priorities, hopes, and dreams; and as it turned out, we had not only planned for many years to achieve these goals, we had acted on those plans.

You might say we did know where we were going, in the same way that I was clear about my desire to put my thoughts about retirement on paper for the benefit of others. What I was not as clear about was the dotting of i's and the crossing of the t's that would have allowed me to avoid a technical disaster with my rough draft. Remember the warning about "sweating the small stuff?" We had done well on the big picture issues, but we were receiving lower marks on the small stuff. Knowing what I had not bothered to learn about the technicalities of the retirement process would have been similarly helpful in eliminating many of the pitfalls of this next phase of life. Another teachable moment? Trial and error? Learning by doing and learning especially from our mistakes would be the order of the day, I guess.

In closing this chapter, I would remind you that if you do not know where you are going, but you care about your destination, you should begin with the First Pillar of retirement planning by answering the Five Ws. It can serve as a helpful outline for the start of your retirement planning. Asking the right questions allows you to start working on the right task. Your retirement years are not a good time to find yourself wandering around looking for the answers to important questions.

o⊸ Key Reminders

~ *Why* do we want to retire—personal reasons, work-related reasons, financial reasons, health reasons, timing reasons—and am I ready for this transition mentally, financially, and personally? How about my spouse's readiness for my retirement?

~ If married, should we question whether we should both retire at the same time? *Who* should retire in our household and is there a good reason for one of us to continue to remain in the workforce for additional income, benefits, or personal timing?

~ *When* should we retire? What is the best timing for us given our retirement benefits, Social Security benefits, health coverages, personal readiness, and a plan for retirement?

~ *Where* should we retire so we can enjoy all the things we hope to do that helped us answer the *Why* questions for retirement?

~ *What* do we plan on doing in retirement given that in the retirement years every day is just like Saturday, unless you have a plan or happen to love Saturdays?

~ Your job is to make the plan and then work the plan.

~ Once you know your destination, pay attention to the details that will get you there.

02

FOUNDATIONAL PILLARS: COST/BENEFIT ANALYSIS, TIMING, VALUE PROPOSITION, AND CASH FLOW

"The thing about basics is they don't really change—it's the details and the proportions that change...."
—John Varratos

Before we move on to the actual information needed to begin this retirement journey, I want to introduce some concepts that I found useful in discussing and navigating the details of retirement. Some of these concepts may be familiar to you or at least terms and descriptions you have heard used by others. After years using these concepts to make decisions daily as an administrator and problem solver, I have made them a part of my everyday vocabulary, and I have come to view them as integral to the way I think and act. I will not go into excruciating detail about these terms, but I will refer to them from here on as the Foundational Pillars of retirement planning.

In discussing retirement with experts in the field or with friends who are well-informed about retirement issues, you may find that some people use language in discussing retirement decisions or retirement in general that is not familiar to you, even though they may use this vocabulary as if it is the most common terminology which everyone should understand. Do not assume that any lack of familiarity on your part with specific terms is due to a deficiency on your part. Terms such as the ones I use in describing the Pillars actually are more often used in business and not commonly used in regular conversation. So, I will attempt to give you a few simple definitions and examples. Secondly, I will remind you often that you should not accept anything on face value simply because an expert says it. You need to understand what you are being told and not be dazzled by fancy footwork in the guise of professional terminology. If you do not understand something, do not proceed until you do.

Pillar #1 Ask the Right Questions: Why, Who, When, Where, and What

Now we need to identify, more succinctly, some of the additional pillars of the retirement planning process.

Pillar #2 Cost/Benefit Analysis

Cost/Benefit Analysis is the second big picture concept that all retirees need to understand. I have always believed that life is a series of cost/benefit analyses. All choices are made to secure certain benefits, and the challenge in doing any analysis is to figure out whether the cost of the benefit is worth what you will have to "pay" for it. For instance, if you decide to regularly exceed the speed limit, you should never complain when you are asked to pay the fine for speeding or the penalty assessed to your auto insurance. You knew the potential cost for exceeding the speed limit, but you valued the benefit of arriving at your destination earlier even more. You also probably imagined you would not get stopped and that you would arrive on time. This is also called the risk/reward approach to decision-making.

We hope that by providing a few mundane examples of the cost/benefit analyses that we all do regularly, this concept will become regularized for you and become useful to you as a framework for decision-making. For example: When you purchase a new electronic or mechanical device like a phone or a washing machine, you have many opportunities for cost/benefit analysis:

~ Do I go with quality or price? What is the difference in longevity between the expensive model and the discount model? Can I afford the higher quality washer?

~ If I stretch for quality and break the budget, what other things will I be unable to do as a result?

~ Should I purchase warranty insurance? What is the likelihood the product will fail? What is the extra cost of the insurance? Is the cost worth the benefit of my peace of mind? Can I afford to replace the product if it fails or is damaged?

Automobiles also pull us into the world of cost/benefit analysis:

~ When is the best time to trade in my car? If I run this car until it stops, what will the benefit be and what will the cost be of that decision?

~ Should I rent a car/van for our upcoming family trip or drive our own car? What will the wear and tear on our car do to its longevity? What will the per mile cost for the rental be and is the difference worth the cost?

~ Is it cost effective for me to purchase a hybrid or an electric car given the cost of fuel and the possible benefits to the environment?

Finally, there are the business decisions that can be clarified by an objective cost/benefit analysis:

~ Would it be better for us to provide additional health care support for our employees or to give them larger raises? The same dollars will be spent, but is the non-taxed element of support for benefits advantageous for the employee?

~ Is it a better idea to give employees a half day off before a major holiday or give them a holiday bonus?

Many decisions can be clarified to some extent by a cost/benefit analysis. Cost does not necessarily relate only to financial situations. As with our decision on the timing of our retirement, there was little about that decision that was financial. It was both personal and professional. Remember that you can quantify almost anything—you just transfer the quality of a situation or outcome to a quantity scale. If being with family represents a 1 on a scale of 10, then it is at the top of your priorities both qualitatively and quantitatively.

I truly believe that life is an unending series of cost/benefit analyses, and that if you are thoughtful and objective in making them, you will make more informed decisions. The same principles apply to retirement. Because the benefit of retiring earlier than the normal retirement age has certain costs attached, you need to be sure that the benefits of leaving your employment situation early outweigh the costs. If, however, you are planning to experience other benefits in your retirement—travel, time for and with family, or a vacation home—you may need a few more years of income and higher Social Security pay outs to ensure that all this is possible. Therefore, the cost of being able to afford all the benefits you are planning for may be working longer and/or delaying your Social Security benefit payment. That cost/benefit analysis might lead you to believe that currently the cost outweighs the benefit.

For Pam and me, retirement had rarely been thought of as the destination. We loved what we did and felt that the benefit of working through the normal retirement age and delaying what we had casually planned as the date we would retire—some four years earlier—made sense and was worth the cost. Our cost/benefit analysis also factored in what we believed was in the best interest of the organization we served. The costs we faced were not financial; they were personal. We had saved over many years to be able to afford retirement. We believed we were on solid financial ground. The benefit we were seeking in retirement was family time after having committed ourselves full time to our careers. The cost of delaying retirement was less time with our children and grandchildren, and less time for ourselves.

Part of our cost/benefit analysis was to unpack the current state of affairs, i.e. relationships with our children and grandchildren. We also had to factor in where they all were in their lives and what would change in that picture during the next four years. Fortunately, we had created patterns of behavior that ensured that we were in regular contact with our family, and we always had made time to be with them on a rotating schedule for major holidays or special events in all their lives. We had found a way to be there for birthdays, graduations, openings of school musicals, and even important games. They had reciprocated with trips to see us in the summer. As long as we could sustain our commitment to family (benefit), we could manage the cost.

The benefit of staying on four extra years was that we derived great energy and personal satisfaction from the work we were doing together. Pam was a full partner in the running of the school, and our work together was exceedingly meaningful to both of us. Believe me, if she or I had believed that the family piece needed attention, we would have seen that as the most important variable in the decision about when to retire. Therefore, the cost/benefit analysis helped us understand that the cost of retiring at age 66 (the normal retirement age for both of us) did not outweigh the benefit, so we could choose what we believed would work best for us.

Pillar #3 Timing

Pam's and my cost/benefit analysis of when to retire was deeply tied to timing. We would be making a decision that would impact not only us but our families, a school community, and in some ways our entire alumni body. Our decision had possible ramifications for thousands of people. Timing, therefore, was a major factor.

This may not be as true for anyone whose work is more independent in nature, but for many people when you retire has an impact on your job, on fellow workers, on the organization, or on your customers. The timing of your exit from the scene matters. Just as the timing of any important decision matters in the regular course of business, it really matters in retirement—in planning for retirement, in saving for retirement, and in determining your transition process and date.

When I was an administrator, I was well known for using quotations from important, classic works I had studied and taught that resonated with me and were applicable to many situations. One of these constructs came from Shakespeare's *Hamlet*: *Ripeness is All*. Of all the important messages or concepts embedded in that play, this was the one that spoke to me most loudly as a young teacher and as a more seasoned professional.

While I will not get into the nuances of the quotation in the play, for me this concept became extremely important in decision-making. Ripeness in this case may be referring to the decay Hamlet saw everywhere around him, and, consequently, the degree of ripeness helped him decide on the course of action he would need to follow in order to address responsibly the death of his father. The ripeness of the situation was inevitably forcing his hand to do something, but the timing of his actions had to be right. Ripeness, therefore, became my code word for timing; and I developed the habit, or, if you will, the discipline of looking at timing as an important element in any decision.

This all made sense to me because the consideration of timing was always an important variable in making any administrative decision or, for that matter, most personal decisions. Timing matters. Consider these situations:

- ~ When do I make an important announcement?
- ~ When do I make a major purchase?
- ~ When do I ask someone to marry me?
- ~ When do I leave one job for another opportunity?
- ~ When should I begin to draw Social Security?

- When do I need to sign up for disability insurance?
- When do I determine I no longer need life insurance?

And of course, when do I retire? The timing of our announcement to retire would have an impact on so many others that we felt the need to apply this Pillar of decision-making to the question. Retirement is all about timing, and as I have been fond of saying during my four decades of leadership and service, "Ripeness is all." It's timing, timing, timing!

Pillar #4 Your Value Proposition

You have probably concluded that any cost/benefit analysis resides comfortably and necessarily with timing. When to do something is part of the cost/benefit analysis, i.e. if we do this now, what are the costs and the benefits of the timing? The value proposition is similarly linked.

I first discovered the concept of the value proposition as I was learning about the creation of mission statements for organizations. An essential part of any mission statement is the goals and objectives statement. When you are describing that "picture on the front of the puzzle box," that is, what you envision your organization (or your retirement) to be; you need to anchor it to your goals and objectives. Goals express what you aspire to be, and the objectives articulate what you value in principle that will guide your processes as you work toward your goals. Your mission statement serves as your vision statement, and it describes to anyone who is reading it what your value proposition is.

Your value proposition explains to anyone considering your product what value the customer will derive from your services or goods, and, more generally, what value you are guaranteeing to the person who buys what you are selling. This is commonly referred to as the value-added of your product; and as with any decision, choices to do one thing as opposed to another have to tie into one's value proposition. Your value proposition as you enter retirement is all about you and your goals and objectives. What do you value and how does what you plan to do advance that value proposition? It links nicely with cost/benefit analysis and timing, because decisions you make about the benefits of certain decisions or the best timing all need to support your value proposition.

Coming out of the school world Pam and I had spent years looking at and creating mission statements for our organizations and discussing our value propositions. A school cannot conduct an effective admissions program unless it can explain to the families who are applying for admissions what the school will promise to provide for their students. That may be why so many schools have similar mission statements. Almost all schools promise to educate the whole child—mind, body, and spirit—for a life of service and productive activity. Most include their commitment to teaching their students teamwork, respect, and cooperation. Finally, they promise academic rigor, athletic opportunity, and diverse environments in which to learn and grow. More specific than the overarching statement of mission are the goals and objectives that are more measurable. "Goal number one is to attract a talented and diverse group of students who will contribute to and benefit from this rich learning environment."

An example of an objective might be that "we will place all our graduates in colleges and universities that represent a good 'fit' for them upon graduation." Usually, mission statements are not subject to change, while the goals and objectives may evolve as programs become more mature. The outcomes from all of this represent the value proposition for the school. What value will you as a parent derive from this experience?

The value proposition for most people paying for private or parochial schools, sending their children to Charter schools, or selecting the best of the area public high schools is that they are signing their children up for an experience that will give them the intellectual tools and personal traits that will position them well for success later in life. They value education deeply and they believe this decision will ensure better educational and personal outcomes for their children later in life.

Our value proposition for retirement was similarly straight-forward. We listed all the things we valued and were willing to sacrifice for, and we considered these the activities or commitments that would guide our thinking and, therefore, our decision-making in retirement. Time with and for family was a value for us. Committing to time with and for each other as a married couple was a goal. Serving others in community service and through our charitable giving was an important objective. Being in a healthy environment with access to the out-of-doors was another goal.

We might have determined that travel answered the need for time together and provided the good vibes necessary for health and prosperity, but travel did not provide the value-added that living in a small town close enough to our children for easy ins-and-outs, and to outdoor recreation, provided. By having a clear value proposition, we were able to prioritize and evaluate the cost/benefit of a variety of decisions. Just as a school is guided by its mission statement in determining how its assets will be spent, a retiree or a retired couple can use a value proposition as a guide to achieve their goals.

You might be tempted to conflate the concept of a value proposition with the answer or answers to the why should I retire question or to the what do I plan to do in retirement question. The Why questions should lead you to discussions that are both practical and philosophical. The What question may be more of a Goals and Objectives, or even a wish-list, at least at first. Your mission statement, which undergirds your value proposition, outlines literally what your value-driven proposition is for your retirement. Just as a school promises what it will do for your children, you are making your intellectual and emotional commitments to what will drive your retirement decisions.

Reminders about value propositions:

~ It is exactly what you would expect to receive from a product or experience.
~ It is the quality of the experience advertised by the person offering the service or product.
~ It is your belief in the quality of the service or experience.
~ In this case there is no person offering you or selling you retirement; you are responsible for the value or quality of the experience.

The value proposition simply serves as another framework for decision-making. Think about the value propositions for the cars you purchase, the home improvement stores you visit, or the non-profits you support—each offers a proposition about its value-added that convinces you to purchase or support it.

One of the most recognizable value propositions is the one that Starbucks offered to its customers: buy and consume our product in our stores and you will get the benefit not only of an excellent cup of coffee, but also a wonderful and enjoyable experience while consuming your coffee. Their value proposition is their offer of what you will get in exchange for purchasing their product in their stores. And remember, we refer to it as a proposition because it is a deal you make with the person creating and offering the experience. In the case of your retirement, you are creating the terms of the experience.

Then translate that concept to you and your retirement. I remember many times having to remind myself and others that all decisions we made for our school need to support and advance the mission and the value proposition. So, think of your retirement being guided by a set of values and principles that remind you always why you are doing what you are doing. In this case, as you enter retirement, you might consider drawing up your own mission statement to guide you and keep you on track toward realizing your goals and objectives. They will help you remain true to the analysis you did when answering the Five Ws.

If you have a clear value proposition guiding you, it can serve as your North Star, helping you navigate the tough decisions and helping you stay anchored to the goals you set for yourself. This does not mean that your goals and objectives will remain the same throughout your retirement; however, having them ensures that they will prompt the right and best questions to guide those new decisions. Remember that "if you don't know where you are going, any path will take you there." This is not a viable way to approach retirement. You need to have a goal and a plan to get you to that destination, and if the decision about the value-added is valid, the plan to get you there is worth paying attention to. The plan should tie directly into your value proposition—which is what retirement is going to provide for you; how to use cost/benefit analysis to support your decision-making; and how to include the variable of timing in your decision-making matrix.

Pillar #5 Cash Flow

The last of the Foundational Pillars, or frameworks, is cash flow. Cash flow describes the amount of cash that is coming into your household that you get to spend on your expenses as a retiree. Cash flow is not what you make; it is more literally what you get to spend. If you think about gross income vs. net income, gross income is the total of all the income sources before taxes and fees; while your net income is what you have left after taxes and fees, income that you have at your disposal for paying your expenses in retirement.

I will devote additional time to this concept later in this book, and I will refer to cash flow from time to time throughout the book to attempt to hammer home the importance of this foundational pillar of retirement. I will go as far as saying that if you do not master the basics and nuances of cash flow, you will not be able to navigate the waters of retirement comfortably and confidently.

Now, we can begin to introduce some retirement specifics which I believe will lead you to other important questions you and those who support you need to answer. This book is intended to assist you in forming the right questions to ask to ensure you are doing the right job as you prepare for and live out your retirement years.

⌐ Key Reminders

~ Cost/benefit analysis is a useful decision-making tool.

- Cost/benefit analysis is also a helpful framework for evaluating retirement decisions.
- The cost of nearly anything can be quantified.
- The benefit of an action or activity can also be quantified.
- If the cost has a payback that is short term—under six years—it is worth considering; i.e. you should be encouraged to take a long-term view if you have the flexibility.
- Paying attention to your value proposition in retirement is tantamount to being true to yourself…and to sticking to the plan.
- Timing decisions need to take into consideration a variety of factors like the impact on you and others.
- Losing sight of timing can result in the right action at the wrong time—like Social Security distributions or retirement dates—which translates into wrong action.
- Cash flow matters.

03

ASSESSING YOUR CURRENT SITUATION

"When is the best time to plant a tree?"
"Twenty years ago!"
"I didn't plant a tree twenty years ago;
so, when is the second, best time?"
"Today!"
—Bill Kelly, Financial Planner in Boston

Now that you realize or have decided that retirement planning is essential, and you have asked some basic yet important questions to point you in the direction that makes the most sense for you; you need to determine how well you are doing now and whether you are taking advantage of all of the best practices of retirement planning. There are so many resources available to you today that were not a part of Pam's and my world when we began to question what we needed to do for retirement and when we should start. There was no internet, no Google, and certainly no constant barrage of sales pamphlets bombarding us with someone's version of best practices. We did not even have AARP because we were too young to qualify. Our parents were not in the habit of sharing their thinking on how they would manage financially or psychologically in retirement, so we had few role models. Smith Barney, Fidelity, Vanguard, TIAA-CREF, and others were just beginning to understand the power of marketing. Therefore, I would have answered the tree planting question as did the person in the ad if it had not been for a business manager at our first school who mentored me in all matters financial. I was thirty-five at the time.

His first lesson was to teach me about the compounding effect/magic of interest. His advice: open a tax-deferred, supplemental retirement account (SRA) now. From his perspective, that was Job #1. Use the regulation on tax-deferred savings plans to your advantage as you work to prepare for retirement, he advised. So, I guess we did plant a tree 20 years ago, and we continued to plant them yearly. (Note: There were no Roth IRAs at the time.)

I also received some good, basic advice from a seminar on financial planning in general and retirement planning specifically, hosted by Smith Barney/Shearson Investments 30 years ago, just as I was stepping into the role of CFO:

~ Set goals—you need goals
~ Determine your objectives
~ Develop and implement a strategy
~ Monitor the strategy
~ Adjust as necessary

Sound familiar—A personal mission statement with its goals and objectives. Clearly, the basics of the game have not changed too much since then; but even with as little information as was in the public domain at that time, 30 years later too many Americans are still relatively unprepared for retirement, or at least they believe they are.

First, let me assure you that today there is no dearth of information or advice coming to and aimed at retirees; and much of it is helpful. The trick is to have a good filter to sift out self-interest from what's in your interest. For example, the question and answer about planting a tree posed above is, I believe, the brainchild of an experienced and, yes, caring financial planner who served the greater Boston area and even the larger New England region for decades. It is, however, just one example of the volleys of targeted sales pitches retirees receive from AARP, TV and radio ads, and weekly mailings on life insurance, annuities, reverse mortgages, medical insurance, and even investment opportunities in gold and silver. Many of these financial planners not only host their own radio shows, but they also underwrite other programming that represents ideologies they support.

In the tree planting scenario, the approach was to encourage all those listening—mostly retirees, I would imagine—not to worry if they have waited too long before getting into the financial markets and, therefore, have not benefitted from the Eighth Wonder of the World—compounding interest. He reminds them that if they missed their chance 20 years ago, they still have access to planning and opportunity through his firm. So, if they have saved at least a responsible amount of money (between $250,000 and $500,000) his advisors/salespeople will meet with them for a personal review of their finances and retirement plans at no cost. This is actually a good offer if you have the personal discipline to listen carefully, take good notes, and postpone making any commitment to action until after you leave the room. Remember, these are professional sales people as well as good financial minds. Tread carefully, however, when any free lunch is offered.

Then there is the *Just Don't Lose the Money* radio program where every discussion or example the talk show hosts highlight starts with the premise that "Rule #1 is just don't lose the money, and Rule #2 is don't forget Rule #1." This advice is reminiscent of Warren Buffett, but maybe he never trademarked the saying, so using the concept was fair game. The theme of this show is that retirement is about the preservation of capital, so you should never take unnecessary risks with the principal of your retirement savings. There can be little argument about that as a general principle, but it is an overly simplistic way of looking at the challenge of making your retirement money last as long as it's needed. As with so many commercials, these sales pitches represent teasers—just enough information to lure you into the private consultation where they get to convince you of their expertise in serving your needs. The ideas might be helpful, but they should be taken with the proverbial grain of salt.

The challenge is realizing that these shows are in reality paid commercials…and in the spirit of full disclosure, they announce at the start of every show that they are precisely that, advertisements for financial products. That does not, however, make them less instructive or educational, but it does remind us that the people on air have purchased this time so they can sell you a service or a product. They use as examples the common problems of retirees who call in to the show to highlight their hosts' expertise. Many of the programs can be helpful, so if you are a talk show listener and enjoy the research part of picking through lots of material embedded in this type of commercial to salvage a few gems, you could do worse than to use these Q & A dialogues as part of your education. My advice is that there is value in the responses to questions from others who may be facing situations similar to yours. You can learn new concepts, and you may be reminded of additional questions you should ask.

The Retirement Review Net Worth Calculation

Now, if your answer was that you did not plant that tree 20 years ago, your focus now has to be on what you have done and/or can continue to do to prepare for retirement. The simple approach is first to make a list of the assets you possess, the debts you have, and your total net worth, that results when you subtract your debts from your total assets. The key is to be thorough. Most peoples' assets may include some of the following:

ASSETS

~ The appraised value of their primary residence.

~ The appraised value of a second home or properties.

~ The appraised value of any land or buildings they own.

~ Their 401(k) or 403(b) retirement and supplemental retirement plan amounts.

~ The amount of other investments.

~ The value of cars or other vehicles.

~ The value of personal possessions e.g. jewelry, furnishings, artwork, or collections.

~ The amount of personal savings accounts.

~ The face value or investment value of whole life insurance policies.

~ The value of any agreements that are in place that ensure future payments.

Once you have totaled these assets, you then need to compile a list of the total of all debts to subtract from the value of your assets. Remember that your net worth is the amount of value you have when you subtract the total of all debts and financial obligations from the total amount of assets. Debts that most people carry include the list below:

LIABILITIES

~ Amount of mortgage remaining on a home.

~ Amount of car or equipment loans.

~ Amount of credit card debt.

~ Amount of any borrowing from retirement accounts or insurance policies.

~ Amount representing personal loans or commitments that need to be paid back.

This approach is exactly the same as the one used by financial planners who work with clients on their planning for the future and specifically for retirement. It does not mean that you are preparing to sell your home or your cars and furnishings or jewelry. The math here is important because this total net worth serves as the foundation for your understanding of where you are in your planning. People often look at their retirement accounts—sometimes even daily—as the proxy for how they are doing as they move toward retirement. This is an important piece of the puzzle, but it is hardly the final word. Remember that issues like mortgages or debts can consume a significant amount of retirement savings during the retirement years. You can have a healthy and growing Individual Retirement Account (IRA) or 401(k)/403(b) plan (employer retirement accounts, also called Qualified Funds because they qualify as tax-deferred vehicles approved by the Government), but you still need to determine how long your retirement plan dollars will last in light of what your expenses and commitments will be in your retirement. Therefore, you need to know where you stand with respect to your net worth, so you understand how much of what you own can be monetized to support your lifestyle costs after you retire.

The result of this first, investigative step will be to give you a baseline for the future. If you have been careful and disciplined about saving and not loading up on debt, you should be happily surprised. If you have lived beyond your means—spending more than you have earned and building up large amounts of credit card debt or bank and personal loans—you are going to need an about-face and a change in the way you live. One thing you will hear often on these call-in shows is how many people did not plant that proverbial tree 20 years ago and are now worried about their retirement savings and are concerned that they might have to work longer before they retire so they can, indeed, afford to retire.

Tax-deferred and Taxable Opportunities

I think the more important question to answer is whether you are doing all you can to maximize your balance sheet (net worth calculation) between now and when you retire. There are some obvious places to begin. If you are employed and your employer has a 401(k) or 403(b) retirement plan, you need to be enrolled. If the plan has a matching component, you need to be taking advantage of that match. Those 403(b) or 401(k) matching funds are referred to as free money, and it's always a good thing to take advantage of free money. These self-funded contributions to your employer plans provide as much of a boost to your retirement dollars as any additional mortgage payments support your paying down of your mortgage balances. This is a calculation of the compounding of interest again, and compounding interest, whether it is working for you (investments) or against you (mortgages), adds up quickly.

You may also have the opportunity to participate in a Roth IRA Plan in which you pre-pay taxes on the money you put away in your IRA or employer-sponsored plan, so it can then grow and later in life be distributed to you tax-free. The real benefit of the Roth concept comes years later when you actually withdraw the money—in retirement—after allowing it to grow tax-deferred from when you deposited it until you draw it out as a retiree. Once again, the concept is to front-end load the tax payment, so you have more reliable and higher cash flow in retirement.

There are additional questions that need to be asked and answered about whether a Roth makes sense for you, and I will come back to this issue as part of the tax efficiency and challenges of taxation in retirement discussion in a later chapter. For now, I would recommend that every employee do her or his homework before deciding the Roth IRA question. This Roth question is another perfect example of the need to ask the right questions and then to do one's homework before making decisions that will have a long-term impact.

If you are self-employed, you will not have the benefit of an employer paying money into your retirement plan or matching a portion of what you contribute to these plans, but the Tax Code does allow you to set up your own plan, referred to as a SEP—a Self-Employed Plan—and you would be missing an opportunity if you did not pause to consider the cost/benefit analysis of contributing to your SEP account. An example may be helpful.

Here are three questions one should ask about self-funding a retirement plan:

- ~ Are tax-deferred opportunities (e.g., retirement plans like IRAs or 401ks and 403bs) always superior to taxable accounts (e.g., after-tax investment or savings accounts)?
- ~ What is the most strategic use of my capital/net revenue in building for the future?
- ~ What is the value of splitting available cash between taxable and tax-deferred investments for retirement purposes?

Clearly, my analysis is intended to lead you to question every assumption you have about tax-deferred and taxable assets in retirement. There are certain constraints in retirement planning when considering how IRAs and taxable savings are treated in actual retirement. No one knows what the tax code will look like in 15, 20, or even 30 years. Secondly, it is a fair assumption that every tax-deferred dollar you have saved or realized from investing will be taxed at some point. The Government will get its tax payment somehow. Required Minimum Distributions (RMD) after age 70½ can complicate one's tax planning in retirement. I do not have all the answers to these questions, but I do know that putting all one's eggs into a single basket can be a mistake. You also need to learn as much as you can about the rules and regulations, and sometimes the opportunities, available to you. So, the question here may be whom do I ask to get the best advice on creating both tax-deferred and non-taxable assets as I save for retirement?

As an example, when Pam and I made the decision to retire at age 70, we had no idea that by making the decision to stay employed until age 70, we would basically be closing a window open to those who are between retirement age (66) and the time when they have to begin to take their RMDs (the year of or the year after you turn 70½) during which you can convert your tax-deferred funds into Roth IRAs by paying the taxes up front. This may not usually be a good idea for tax-planning reasons, but it is a question that should not go unanswered, or worse yet, unasked. And if it goes unasked, it may represent an opportunity cost in your individual case.

There is also a strategy you can employ of managing carefully the taking down of your tax-deferred funds so you do not get hit with larger RMDs after the deadline surrounding 70½, which could complicate your tax planning. Once again, I would not have made a different determination about when we retired, given our analysis, but it would have been helpful to have all the information in front of us so we could have asked and answered the right questions, and have done a full cost/benefit analysis.

As I trust you are beginning to see, you need to determine what the right questions are and then what the cost/benefit analysis suggests, what appears to be the best timing for the decision, whether the value proposition is being served, or how your cash flow will be impacted depending on the decisions you make. Also, factor in your personality and tendencies in making your decisions. For instance, if you are not disciplined about saving for the rainy day and are likely to spend savings that are not tied up in a qualified retirement plan which cannot be accessed without a penalty, you need to be honest about that and choose the safer route by locking into the qualified, tax-deferred plan. If, on the other hand, you are someone who is extremely self-disciplined about saving and spending, you may have more flexibility in your investment options. Which are you? This is important information to factor into such decisions.

To bring this section to a close, let's add to the list of questions that need to be answered in preparation for retirement:

~ What does my net worth analysis indicate the things I need to do next?

~ How can I make the best decision on the type/s of savings vehicles to use—tax-deferred, taxable, other vehicles?

~ What do I need to know about self-employed savings strategies (SEPs), if they apply to me?

~ How can I best educate myself about finance and investments for the near and long term?

~ Am I building the right number of assets and in the right categories (taxable, tax-deferred, inflation-protected) for retirement?

~ Do I need a plan for restricting or controlling the amount of debt I have accumulated?

This is a part of your financial preparation for retirement. I am reminded of the fable of the ant and the grasshopper. The ant worked tirelessly preparing itself for the coming winter. The grasshopper on the other hand, lay in the sun, fiddling (literally and figuratively) blissfully unaware or unconcerned about the future. When the winter came, the ant was fully prepared, warm, fed, sheltered. The grasshopper, on the other hand, was in trouble: no home, no food supplies, and no prospects, except, of course, his dependence on the charity of others. And the moral of the story is the question—yet another important question—for you to answer: Which describes you? And if your answer is the grasshopper, then what do you need to do to become the ant...with a beautiful, 20-year-old tree next to your anthill? Warren Buffett, whom we will now give credit for his wisdom, put it this way:

"Someone is sitting in the shade today because someone planted a tree a long time ago."

o⌐ Key Reminders

~ The best time to plant a tree was 20 years ago simply because compounding interest is the Eighth Wonder of the World.

~ Time is much more important than money when it comes to investing.

~ Financial plans start with objective net worth analysis.

~ Tax-deferred vehicles offered by employers, like 401(k) and 403(b) plans, allow you to grow your savings tax-deferred until age 70½. That can be a huge benefit.

~ Matching contributions—where employers match a percentage of or sometimes even dollar for dollar what you put toward your retirement—are tantamount to free money.

~ If possible, make certain you consider funding both tax-deferred retirement plans and after tax, or taxable, savings plans. Balance and flexibility matter in retirement.

~ Remember Uncle Sam will get his tax-bite when qualified money is finally paid out.

~ Make sure to understand your Required Minimum Distributions (RMD) schedule to leverage the tax-deferred savings they can provide and to help with tax-efficiency.

04

THE IDEAL SCHEDULE
FOR RETIREMENT PREPARATION

---

*"If you had your choice of whether you
would rather have either time or money to
plan for retirement, you should choose time."
"The rich invest in time. The poor
invest in money."*
—Warren Buffett

Saving for retirement is a multi-faceted process and should take years. Reference the 20-year-old tree. Therefore, if we were laying out the ideal approach, we would advise you that planning for retirement is something you should approach decade by decade.

30 years out

In a perfect world if you were to take your retirement pulse and check the meter on when you would prefer to retire, that would be happening about three decades before you reach the retirement age for your generational cohort. As guidance we can apply the oft-used investment calculation that shows us if we put away $1,000 a year from age 30 to age 45, invested it in index funds, let it grow, and did not touch it until retirement; we would have more money saved from those 15 years of saving than if we put away that same $1,000 yearly in the same investment for the 25 years from 40-65, as long as the returns were the same. The reason: compounding interest. You are building not just on the principal of $1,000 each year for 15 years; rather, you are getting your return on both the principal and the interest it earns until retirement, which is actually 35 years—age 30-65—in the first instance compared to the interest and principle for 25 years if you begin at age 40.

20 years out

Your second check point would ideally be at the 20-year mark before your retirement, and at that time you should revisit your thinking about retirement timing and make certain you are building your asset and retirement profile as you had planned and then formatting the right questions. Remember, you make the plan; then work the plan. After that, you should evaluate the progress of the plan. You also should be factoring in health and family circumstances. Retirements are as individual as people, and every situation demands personalized attention.

Questions of mitigating risk in your professional and personal life should be paramount at this checkpoint. If something were to happen to you on the path to a successful retirement, would you be prepared for that contingency? Are you on track to realize the goals you have articulated for yourself? Are you continuing to educate yourself about investment opportunities, federal benefit programs that will apply to you, and insurances that may give you the security you desire and need?

If the answers to these questions are affirmative, you can "Pass Go and Collect $200." If you are missing your targets or have different challenges to address, you need to recalibrate. Twenty years out is a good time to revise the schedule. Remember, time is your greatest ally in the retirement game.

10 years out

When you reach the last decade before retirement, your third checkpoint, you need to begin the next stage of the retirement education process. At this juncture it is not simply a matter of checking in quarterly on your retirement funds and retirement plans to be certain the balance of investments is correct; it is time to investigate exactly how they work. For those in corporations or schools, the Human Resources Office is a great resource. If you are self-employed, you might consider a financial planning professional to support you, or at least become very familiar with the internet's financial planning tools and articles. For either of these situations, consulting regularly with the bank or financial firm that holds your money is a good place to start. Most financial firms have education materials on their websites, and they are quite good. Educating yourself is a critical part of successful planning. You simply cannot go forward making decisions about something as important as retirement if you do not understand the components of your plans, contracts, investments, and entitlement benefits, e.g. Social Security and Medicare.

At this 10-year anniversary before retirement, as you count down to your retirement party, you should already have a clear understanding of what the retirement landscape looks like. You also, fortunately, will still have time to reroute. As with your car's GPS, if you missed a turn or took a wrong turn, you can reroute and get back on track well in advance of your planned retirement date. Or in a worst-case scenario, you might have to take a longer route and delay your arrival at your destination, remembering to obey the speed limit—cost/benefit analysis really applies here. There is no such thing as a get-rich-quick scheme.

Your retirement savings check-up a decade out is absolutely important, but you also need to broaden your thinking at this point to include the replacement not just of income but also of the health and welfare benefits you will need and want during your retirement years. These ten years will be your "measure twice and cut once" period.

I wish Pam and I had been more aware of the opportunity as well as the obligation we had to ask and answer the right questions about many of the details of retirement benefits. Our view of retirement was far too simplistic. How complicated could this be? "Old" people are retiring in great numbers every year, and people with a lot less training than we had in compensation, pension program details, and retirement benefits seemed to be completing this task seamlessly. There were so few moving parts, or to continue the puzzle box picture analogy, not all that many pieces. I had made up a list of To Do's for my employees 30 years ago and in retrospect they still seemed to apply to today's retirement planning climate:

- ~ Know the value of your total compensation package (Salary and benefits).
- ~ Know what you spend and control it (i.e. don't let it control you).
- ~ Develop a plan for regular savings—find a reason and a way to save.
- ~ Use tax-deferred savings if and when possible.
- ~ Save at least 10% of your salary every year.

While all the above recommendations still apply, in revisiting this list and preparing a similar list as a retiree 30 years later, I would add to and amend this earlier list to read as follows:

~ Know the value of your total compensation package.
~ Know what you spend, and control it.
~ Develop a plan for regular savings.
~ Take advantage of the tax-deferred opportunities you have but do not dismiss the importance of taxable savings or Roth accounts.
~ Increase your savings goal from 10% to 15% of your income, if possible.
~ Remember there are a variety of ways to save, so this does not mean only saving by using the stock market. Sometimes investing in yourself makes equal or more sense.
~ Respect and understand the value and importance of compounding interest and the helpful Rule of 72. (If you get a 6% return on your money, it will double in 12 years (6 x 12 = 72). Divide 72 by your rate of return and you get the number of years it takes to double your investment.) If you use a less-well-known Rule of 115, that is the number needed to triple an investment.
~ Never take advice from anyone who wants to sell you a product rather than simply selling you advice.
~ Keep things simple and don't invest in anything you don't understand.

The Simplistic View of Retirement

I assumed Pam and I already knew most of the best practices for investing, but I made the mistake of believing that finances were the *sine qua non* of retirement preparation. The rest of the puzzle pieces were few, simply explained, and easily enacted. All you had to do was follow the basic principles:

~ You sign up for Social Security.
~ You replace your medical insurance with a personal medical insurance policy.
~ You determine what other, if any, insurances you need to replace what you had when employed.
~ You decide what you want to do in the next 25 to 30 years of retirement.
~ You draw from your IRAs and your personal savings to pay for your retirement lifestyle.

If you are reading this and were more attuned to the importance and complexity of these steps and more attentive to the nuances of each of these actions, you already realize that there are many choices within each of these categories that you will have to make, and important outcomes with which you will have to live. As it turned out with my not so nuanced view about protecting my work product on the computer, there was much I needed to know that I had little idea would ever be an issue.

o⟲ Key Reminders

~ Ask yourself the hard questions about the future and then do something to ensure the success you are planning for.
~ Keep yourself on a decade-by-decade—30, 20, 10 years out—checklist for retirement actions that need following.

- ~ Understand the time-value of money—compounding interest and the Rule of 72.
- ~ Time is a critical asset in life and in investing.
- ~ Create an evergreen plan so you can stay flexible.
- ~ Don't underestimate the complexity of retirement and act accordingly—plan and save wisely.

05

CASH FLOW AND TAX EFFICIENCY

"Never take your eyes off the cash flow because it is the life blood of business."
—Richard Branson

I wish someone had told me in the most basic terms that retirement is essentially an exercise in cash flow and cash management. As a financial guy I understood the concept of cash flow. In its most elementary state, cash flow is the amount of money that moves in and out of your business, organization, or life in the course of a month or a year. For a company cash flow is the money that is generated from the business which is used to pay the bills, fund the repair and replacement, and reinvest in the business. There may be other forms of benefit accruing to the company, but cash flow deals only with cash. Furthermore, your net profit after all the cash is in is a statement of how much cash is left at the end of the month that the company gets to keep. It's what you have left after all of your obligations have been paid… or simply stated, profit.

This is essentially what retirement is—an exercise in cash flow. If you have planned well, and if you were lucky enough to be with an employer who had a generous retirement plan, you have monthly income. You have cash flow, and from that cash, you have the capacity to pay the bills and arrange for the maintenance of your home and lifestyle.

I had thought retirement planning was about reaching some magic number. After all, we had been protected from many of the everyday expenses because of our school lifestyle. Our challenge was to translate what our life had been like within the boarding school bubble into a more realistic view of what life would be like for the average retired couple. My data points on this subject were few. As school people leaving the protected environment we had lived in for 47 years, we had not been part of a world where people shared their thoughts about retirement very openly. There was a great deal of retirement material coming our way as we closed in on the magic date, but we had precious little real-world experience. I certainly understood the business concept of cash flow, but I did not know it applied to retirement.

Many of our friends owned their own businesses and continued working in, or at least overseeing the businesses from the owner's box through their retirement dates. They still had a place to go to daily and a stream of income for the retirement each had hoped to enjoy.

My fixation on a number was fueled by the commercials I had seen, the most recent of which was, ironically, a Prudential Life TV ad which showed people walking on a grid measuring how long their retirement savings would last them in retirement. As you would expect, not many got beyond the halfway point, and the inference was that there were insurance products—maybe even annuities—to address every retirees' financial concerns.

Some commercials targeting retirees discussed the benefits of trading in one's retirement vehicles for cash. There was even one commercial that showed an older couple who were discussing the benefits of selling back their insurance policy—or parts of that policy—to insurance companies interested in buying the payout benefit or the cash value in the policies. This might have suggested that the couple had insurance they no longer needed but now had the chance to monetize. This may have been a strategy to trade up for cash, but it certainly represented a strategy that should not have been entered into casually. Actually, this would have been the perfect time for a cost/benefit analysis and a conversation on timing.

Another commercial suggested that monetizing your home by engaging in a reverse mortgage was a responsible way to leverage the value of your home or possibly to monetize it. You had the opportunity to reverse your mortgage by accepting a payment or a series of payments which would be deducted from the value of your home, so you would end up having more of the cash you needed to live in retirement. For a long time, reverse mortgages were considered traps that retirees needed to avoid and that those selling this strategy were using reverse mortgages to prey upon older residents who were unclear about how much they were losing. I believe that of late both insurance policy purchases and reverse mortgages have received more scrutiny and have been constrained by more regulation to ensure that retirees are protected. Still, anyone considering using either insurance policy sales or engaging in reverse mortgages needs to do his or her due diligence to be certain that all the consequences and especially the small print are fully understood. This is another time for a cost/benefit analysis.

Still focused on having a set amount of money—the number—I ached to call someone whose financial profile might be like mine to ask what I believed was the most pressing question for all retirees: What is the number?

There must be a number you can shoot for during your accumulation stages, that when reached, would allow you to call it a day. I was a rational person with business sense. I had learned through most of my life that there were rules of thumb for everything…numbers that led you in the right direction and told a story. I assumed it must be this way for retirement. Then I saw another TV commercial: What is your number? It showed people walking around carrying their numbers. If television extras could have them, why not all retirees? I must have picked up the phone a dozen times to ask a colleague of mine that question. But I never called because I feared this was a complicated question and answer, and I worried that by asking it of someone who had by his own admission, failed retirement, I might be opening a wound, or, worse yet, he might have no rational answer.

Then the golden opportunity presented itself at a casual meeting of a number of former school administrators and financial people. My colleague happened to be in the group. He was now retired for the second time, or semi-retired (his description), so I felt safer treading on the sacred ground. I said, boldly, "I have been wanting to ask you a somewhat personal but important question for some time and wasn't sure the time was right."

He leaned forward, obviously intrigued. "Really?"

"Yes, and now that you are retired…."

"Semi-retired," he added quickly.

"Yes, semi-retired." I said. "Now that you are semi-retired and have settled in to a routine (I was thinking not too settled) can you tell me what the 'number' is?"

"What number?" he asked.

"The number—the number of assets one needs to have in hand to retire successfully." I blurted out.

Just asking the question made me feel both inappropriate and clueless. Then, before he could respond, another colleague at the table offered the answer. Confidently, he said, "80% of your average salary over the last five years of your working years," as if this was something everyone knew. He continued, "If you add together your Social Security income, your payments from your 403b /401k, and any income from IRAs and taxable savings; those annual dollars should be equal to at least 80% of what you were making at the end of your career. That should do you just fine."

"What?" I exclaimed. "That was the formula we used 30 years ago when everyone had a pension plan and annuitized their retirement savings in order to ensure they would get a regular check in the mail monthly. That was when people had a life expectancy of 10 years in retirement, not 25 to 30 years. You can't be serious; the calculation is far more nuanced than that, and as someone with your level of conversancy with numbers and money, you should know better."

"Whoa." he said. "This is just the rule of thumb. This is where you start. The question you ask has no sensible answer. Actually, you're asking the wrong question."

Another shrine was empty. Was there really no answer? Any hints would have been appreciated. This was one of the few questions I could not get an answer to on Google, and since both my parents and Pam's had passed away without revealing the secret, I was getting desperate. Then my prayers were answered, at least I thought they were when I was walking through an airport terminal and happened upon a book advertised as a *New York Times* Bestseller entitled *The Number.* The proverbial clouds parted, the sun broke through, and heavenly music entered my consciousness, all simultaneously. I could not wait to get to the Table of Contents to get my answer. The book was divided into three parts: 'Chasing It,' 'Figuring It,' and, at last, 'Finding It.' I could barely contain myself. I opened the book and I walked off the plane three hours later with a wry grin on my face. I had finally been provided with an answer to my question that made sense. It didn't exactly make me happy, but it gave me important food for thought. I felt a little bit like Dorothy in the *Wizard of Oz*. What I was seeking, I had possessed all along. The answer was somewhat obvious, and the author of *The Number*, Lee Eisenberg, had framed it this way as he ended the last chapter of the book:

"Either way, getting incensed over who has what strikes me as a waste of psychic energy and a waste of time. Better to invest this valuable energy, and use that time, to come to terms with who you are, or, if it better pleases you, to make more money. Others can write books on how to die rich or to die broke. How to die laughing, that's up to you."

So, there was no answer, but my worst fears evaporated right before my eyes; it was up to me. I could never determine the number and, then fully armed with this information, sail blithely off into retirement's sunset. Every retiree was going to have to figure out for him or herself the answer to the really important question: Who Are You? I was somewhat relieved because Pam and I had a strong sense of not only who we were, but also what we wanted to do in retirement and where we needed to be, to be happy. And, ultimately, we were well on our way to understand how we could die laughing? Game on!

Retirement, as it turned out, was actually an exercise in cash flow, not income

We had thought all along that Job #1 was to be clear about what our income in retirement would be. Wrong question! Job #1 is figuring out what you need to spend and then determine whether you have enough after-tax money coming in from a variety of sources to pay for what you spend. This is because it is not what you make, but what you get to keep and spend of what you make, that matters.

For example, people in finance and investment businesses who value the companies they are considering investing in, understand that a critically important part of the valuation is that company's cash flow. If the company sells lots of product for whopping, gross income numbers, but sells them at a very modest profit, and if on top of that income, they need to invest more capital in their business; and, additionally, if they have to then pay high corporate taxes on top of the investments in the future…and then are responsible for paying dividends to their investors; they may not have generated much net income. Indeed, they may even have lost money. Retirement is like that. It is an exercise in cash flow.

Sources of Income in Retirement

First, you need to determine all your sources of income:

- ~ Social Security (for you or for you and your spouse).
- ~ Withdrawals from your 401(k) or 403(b) plans or your IRAs or Required Minimum Distribution (RMDs).
- ~ Withdrawals from any savings you want or need to access.
- ~ Taxable investment accounts withdrawals.

- ~ Pension payments, if applicable.
- ~ Any annuity payments.
- ~ Other sources.

Realities that Erode Income

Then you need to develop the same list accounting for taxes or charges against these funds. For example, you need to account for the fact that depending on your income level in retirement, up to 85% of your Social Security can be taxed. You also need to remember and account for the fact that your 403(b) or 401(k) income and income from your IRAs will be taxed as regular income. The same is true for any pension payments or annuity payments, except Roth IRAs. Uncle Sam will always get his share of tax revenue unless your income is at or below a very modest level. In 2018 that allowable income number at or below which your Social Security, for instance, would not be taxed was $25,000 for a single filer and $32,000 for joint filers. Single filers with a combined income of $25,000–$34,000 would pay income taxes on up to 50% of their Social Security benefits. Those filers with an income of more than $34,000 would have up to 85% of their Social Security benefits taxed. Joint filers making $32,000–$44,000 would pay taxes on up to 50% of their Social Security benefits and on up to 85% if they made more than $44,000.

You also need to remember that if you deduct your Medicare Part B or Parts B and D premiums from your Social Security checks—which will result in a significant discount in the monthly premium—that will also lower your monthly income stream. I remember how good I felt about the amount of income coming in from Social Security monthly and then feeling far less well after I had accounted for the taxes and charges/fees/penalties that would be counted against it.

Now most of those reading this book will react to the above statement of shock that I expressed by saying, "What's new? I have been creating a budget, spending within my means, and balancing my budget for years. So why will retirement be any different?" I would respond quickly that for Pam and me, living in an assisted living arrangement at schools for all of our married lives, had protected us from a number of realities about all of the expenses homeowners and people in the real world have; regardless, for all of us in retirement, there will no longer be a weekly or monthly salary check coming from an employer. There will be no regular check in the mail, except Social Security, or maybe a pension, or possibly distributions from your IRA or 401(k)/403(b). Maybe you will be prepared to set up a responsible income stream from your retirement savings or investments. You probably will be better set up to do these things than we were, but actual, net income can come as a surprise. That is why it is wise to plan.

Normal Expenses in Retirement

The next step is to create a list of monthly, quarterly, bi-annual, and annual expenses. Some of these expenses will represent your cost of living essentials, while others may be programmatic or discretionary. All need to be included on the list. I have created an example below that represented our first iteration of regular and repeatable expenses:

~ Mortgage, if still a factor, or rental costs
~ Electrical costs

- ~ Heating costs
- ~ Trash removal and recycling costs or fees
- ~ Water and sewer costs
- ~ Television, phone, and internet charges
- ~ Medicare costs
- ~ Medical expenses in addition to Medicare, i.e. supplemental insurance and deductibles.
- ~ Pet care
- ~ Dental costs
- ~ Vision costs
- ~ Food
- ~ Gas
- ~ Travel
- ~ Entertainment

Then I had to add the less obvious costs that were not as readily apparent as those above:

- ~ Federal and State taxes
- ~ Property taxes
- ~ Automobile insurance and registration
- ~ Car maintenance
- ~ Home maintenance
- ~ Homeowners' insurance—property/casualty policies
- ~ Personal insurance—long term care policies or life insurance policies

After considering all of this, it becomes even clearer that cash flow is what matters. It also makes a strong case for knowing what is in your budget, being clear about what needs to be there, and being disciplined about the difference between needs and wants, necessities and luxuries. Remember the warning that Peter Drucker voiced when he talked about the challenge of being disciplined about following one's well-laid plans: "Culture eats strategy for breakfast every time!" If you create the right spending culture and maintain that culture, you will be far more likely to succeed in following the strategy you have outlined for your retirement.

There were so many other surprises waiting for us as we entered retirement. As you are now fully aware, we had been if not spoiled at least protected from many of the realities that plague many people throughout their lifetimes but had not been part of our life experience. Mowing the lawn? Done for us. Removing the snow? Also done for us. Recovering lost material from your laptop? Technology Department more than ready to help. Workout and fitness facilities? Lower level of the gym—no charge. Therefore, when our son-in-law opened the trunk of his car and unloaded his used lawn mower and a leaf blower, we were thrilled. Tools for the tasks at hand. I remembered these well from my youth. This would be fun. Until they needed servicing, maintenance, and repair.

We had to replace all our support systems—doctors, estate attorney, dentist, dermatologist, and car dealership. There were many changes, like every day feeling like a Saturday…but thinking about our retirement budget as a cash flow analysis was the real eye opener. When there are no more paychecks coming in the mail, you have to know how your money is being spent and what your net revenue will be on both a monthly and quarterly basis. You learn that everything has a cost and that there is no longer such a thing as a small change. Warren Buffet's advice is worth mentioning:

"Do not save what is left after spending, spend what is left after saving."

⊶ Key Reminders

Your number is not a mythical net worth calculation you need to have saved; it is having the cash flow to do what you need and want to do in retirement.

~ Have a realistic accounting of all your expenditures.

~ Net income and gross income are not the same and the difference can be the difference in being successful in retirement or failing retirement and heading back to work.

06

LEARNING TO NAVIGATE THE HEALTH CARE CRUCIBLE

"There is not one truth, there is only a truth."
—Anon

Ever since I could remember, medical insurance and Blue Cross/ Blue Shield were synonymous and equaled health care. Both schools we served had BC/BS-Anthem plans. The process was simple: you purchased a BC/BS plan; paid for the option that covered as much service as possible; and assumed that you'd have enough savings to pay the deductible. Then you hoped for the best. I didn't have a sophisticated view of how insurance markets worked. I realized that insurance companies negotiated with hospitals and physician groups to set rates for procedures and services that resulted in discounts for the insured. That was the cost. The benefit for the insurance company was volume and, therefore, profit. If enough people used these services, everyone benefited.

Then technology and medical research changed the medical landscape, and the cost of medical services skyrocketed. Insurance companies were forced to create new product lines that helped them and consumers control the cost of care. The fact that this was happening was lost on many people who were not having to make hard decisions about how much of their health risk they wanted to insure. For benefits administrators, however, the picture was becoming increasingly pessimistic and daunting. Employers were faced with the impossible choice of offering affordable health care with responsible and manageable deductibles (which were almost prohibitively expensive for employers) or to allow employees to determine how they wanted to spend their compensation dollars—insuring themselves against health challenges or taking more in salary and rolling the dice on health care costs. People and employers began to realize there was no free lunch, and they knew they could not control health care's rapidly rising costs. Competition among insurance companies increased, and plan administrators began to get as creative as possible about the structure of plans—front end load the cost with high premiums and lower deductibles, or risk more financial challenge if you needed the care by paying lower premiums, loading up on deductibles, and hoping for a healthy future. This is another typical cost/benefit question.

These were the medical insurance and expense wars that led to wellness programs and to a number of highly publicized and politicized health care reform efforts. Again, because there was no free lunch, someone was going to have to assume responsibility for the cost—employers, insureds, or the Government. Regardless of the public or private sector response, someone was going to have to pay. But what could we do as a society or as individuals if we had so many people in the country who could not afford the cost of personal insurance? Who pays for them?

This is not a political statement or a position paper on health care and its challenging history. This is the context that most retirees are challenged to navigate when they leave the work force and enter retirement. As happy or unhappy as they have been as employees who had to choose between high or low deductible plans, HMOs or PPOs, or self-insurance before the Affordable Care Act, and who had to endure changes to new insurance companies who were the low bidder in their employers' annual lottery; or paying for the privilege and convenience of being able to select and retain their doctors; as a retiree, you will be entering the Medicare system, and this is a whole new game—the rules of which you should know before you retire. I wish we had known the right questions to ask.

Naively, Pam and I assumed we would move to New Hampshire and at the right moment transition from our employer-provided plan to a Medicare plan and then purchase a supplemental medical insurance plan to cover the gaps in coverage. Directionally, this was correct. We had made the decision we referenced earlier that we would work beyond age 65, which meant we would not have to make a decision at our normal retirement ages about our Medicare choice. We knew enough to check off the required boxes as we signed up for Social Security and Medicare Part A on our 65th birthdays, but we admit to being surprised that we were asked at that time whether we wanted to also sign up for Medicare Part B. Part B? "Yes," our Social Security representative said, "Part B."

Now, I am certain we had read about the four parts of Medicare or seen ads for products in AARP, but we did not really understand the differences. One plan is for "hospital care" and the other is for doctor's care. Wouldn't there be doctors involved in hospital care? Our helpful Social Security representative then bailed us out by following up with the next question: "Will you be staying on your employer's medical plan or be using Medicare?" Whew. We would be staying on our employer's plan for the next four years thereby avoiding having to answer a question we had not anticipated because we had not done our homework. We had no idea at that time what a black box the entire Medicare process was.

Our ignorance was not a function of there not being enough available information. We had been receiving the AARP publication for years, but we were more focused on the "Your Money" section than the ads for Medicare coverages and the "Your Health" section. We were aware, tangentially, of the political claims that AARP was partial to certain insurance plans and favored certain approaches to health care, but those were uninteresting to a couple like us who were focused mainly on 800 plus teenagers and a school that took the lion's share of our time and interest. So, you can imagine our surprise when as retirees we began to receive regular brochures in the mail and, more intrusively, on our phones, highlighting the benefits of certain insurance companies and programs for Medicare coverages.

We responded as most tech-savvy seniors would—we Googled it. We dialed up Medicare Plans. Literally, within minutes our phones began to ring. Not only were we called; we were sent emails by Medicare insurance brokers who were offering to help. Everyone seemed to be immediately aware of and appropriately concerned about our situation and our obvious need for assistance. And you know what…they were right. We had no idea about the relative complexities. What we learned was that the people who work as general insurance brokers for Medicare are actually very helpful. I have concluded that they all agree to take truth serum. You still need to ask the right questions, but they will answer them truthfully. You just need to go beyond the basic question of comparative price and determine what aspects of the insurance plan are not immediately obvious.

For example, we assumed that we could contact our Blue Cross/Anthem Office and sign up. Not so fast, my friend. We could not get the Anthem representatives to return our calls, and there did not seem to be a reasonable explanation for the non-response. Then we asked the specific question of one of these Medicare sales people and were told that not every insurance company offers policies for Medicare in every state. The sales person added—maybe at the risk of crossing the "don't give any information unless explicitly asked" line—that if we had stayed and resided in Indiana, we would have had access to Anthem coverage, and, actually, we could have received better rates from a number of major insurance companies as Indiana residents than were now available to us as residents of New Hampshire.

Another rule of the road: It is imperative to do the research to determine whether the destination for the moving van is a state that your insurance company of choice does business in. This may also be a part of your cost/benefit analysis. This is one of the investigative questions we should have known to ask when determining the options for health care insurance. We also should have asked and answered the question about the best resources for information on the Medicare process. There are so many sales people who are out there willing to provide information, but you need to consult with someone you know and trust about what questions to ask.

A Case Study in Medical Insurance

The scenario that Pam and I faced serves as a good illustration of the issues and decisions you will face with health care in your retirement years. As is the case with all retirees, we had heard that one of the truly significant challenges of funding one's retirement is and will continue to be health care. Financial advisors, retirement fund representatives, and human resource officers all go out of their way to remind you that you need to plan for high dollar costs for health insurance during retirement. So, imagine my surprise when the first quotes came in from telemarketers at about $150 a month for Part B coverage. (Part A is made available at no cost.) My calculation was that if Pam and I both were on the plan, we would only be paying a fraction of what we had been hearing about as crushing health care costs in retirement. But that was only the cost of Part B. In addition, we learned that if we had Part B but chose not to purchase Part C, we would then need Part D, if we wanted insurance coverage to attenuate the cost of prescription drugs. This was beginning to look like alphabet soup. But, surprisingly, the cost of Part D was only about $22 a month. I did the math: $22 times two is only $44 a month, but then you have to add the cost of the drugs you or your spouse take to the real cost, and that may add significantly to that monthly amount, depending on what tier the drug is categorized as. Carefully, you do the research and realize this is actually quite affordable, and you move on.

On your next call, you make the mistake of trying to get Medicare information from the local Social Security Office because somewhere you read that Medicare and Social Security are inextricably linked. However, you quickly learn that the Social Security administration is not overly helpful on issues other than Social Security benefits. They are willing to explain to you, however, that if you deduct your Medicare insurance monthly premiums from your Social Security check, you will get a discount in the cost of insurance. Who would have figured that out? Not us to be sure.

This all left us wondering if we still did not have the part of the coverage that must be the real costly part, the part that ensured that we would not have unreasonable deductibles. This we learned was called supplemental or Medigap insurance. Once again it would have been helpful to have known all of this before we found ourselves only a few months away from needing the coverage but still without a policy, but we did not. Concerned about our uncertain status, we listed the questions we needed to answer.

- What are the advantages of enrolling in Medicare C?
- How does Medicare C differ from supplemental or Medigap insurance?
- How many choices are there for Medigap plans?
- What are the costs of Part C and Medigap plans?

Now all this is information we should have been aware of in planning for retirement. Even though the landscape changes quickly in this world of health insurance—especially with a change of administration in the White House—it would have been helpful to know more of the basics. Let's continue the case study we began earlier.

Once we dig in to any task, we are relentless. We will have as many conversations as we need to get the right insurance, at the right cost, with the right company. Not so easy. First, we decided we needed to understand what happened to simple, old Original Medicare? Original Medicare is simply-put the combination of Part A (for hospital services) and Part B (for doctor visits, lab work, outpatient services, and preventative care). Remember that Part A is free, but Part B comes with a premium of between $120 and $150 a month depending on your age at retirement and whether you deduct payments from your Social Security checks, a strategy which will save you 20% and is well worth doing. Somehow this needs more attention given to it.

Unfortunately, there are so many twists and turns in the process, it is easy to digress. My apologies. The challenges with Original Medicare relate to the fact that it is a federal program and not one operated by an insurance company, so that is the good news. It will never take its ball and go home. But it might end up costing you more because of deductibles resulting from major medical events. That is the bad news.

So now Part C is on the table. Part C, also called Medicare Advantage, we learn, was only devised recently, in 1997, to compete with the options of HMOs and PPOs that health insurance companies created to keep premiums lower. In the Medicare Advantage Plan you get Part A and Part B from private insurance companies approved by Medicare. The advantage with Part C is that you get your prescription insurance rolled in to the plan so you have what AARP refers to as one-stop shopping. What you also get, unfortunately, are the requirements of the insurance companies' plans that may limit the insured to using certain networks and also create more costly plan structures. This was not sounding positive.

Then we turned our attention to Part D, a concept enacted by Congress in 2003 to support Americans with the cost of prescription drugs in retirement. Part D turned out to be the necessary complement to Part A and Part B if you are choosing the Medigap or supplemental plan. Yet there is a catch. The challenge with Part D is that the plans offered by private insurance companies vary widely, so doing your homework on both the costs and the plan's construction is critical. Another complication with Part D was that if you had not applied for the program when you signed up for Medicare parts A and B, you could be subject to a monetary penalty when you do sign up. By now we had decided that the supplemental plan was in our future, so we made the commitment to Part B and Part D. We still were missing some very important financial information, but we did not yet know enough to ask.

We were making headway on our Medicare coverage now, but there was still this nagging piece of information, suspended like the notorious hanging chad in the Florida Presidential election: the matter of the income adjustment surcharge. Early on in our Medicare process/journey we had spoken with a Medicare sales person who shared with us an estimate for our final of Medicare Part B that was four times as high as any we had been quoted to date. He was hurried in his explanation, but he asked me if I had made more than the allowable threshold in salary the previous year, explaining obliquely we would be paying a surcharge. He indicated that our gross income numbers from our tax returns would be used as the benchmarks the government would factor in determining how much extra Pam and I would have to pay for our Part B Medicare plan. The allowable amount he referenced as the trigger number was much less than my salary for each of the two previous years, but he was not specific about the extra fee/penalty costs charged for making too much money. He also neglected to mention that the same formula for an income surcharge would be applied to our Part D costs. I hadn't forgotten about that conversation, but the subject never surfaced again on any of the conversations with sales people about our supplemental plan costs. I hoped for the best, but I should have remembered that as a good friend of ours was fond of saying, "Hope is not a strategy!"

I recall saying to myself that if this off-hand comment about surcharges were to be true, people's warnings about the cost of health care in retirement may not have been that far off. Not encouraging to say the least.

Now we had to choose a program for our Supplemental/Medigap policy. How hard could this be? How many options are there? TEN! You get to choose from Plans A, B, C D, F, G, K, L, M, or N. Really? Really! The good news turned out to be that just about all versions of the plans are the same…unless of course you live in one of three states, in which case… Remember: always read the fine print. All of it. And be prepared to ask the right questions.

The reality is that these choices are not that hard to make, but if we had known more about how the system worked, we could have been assured of making the right decisions for us up front and planning for them rather than guessing and hoping. Remember, "set the plan, then work the plan."

In our case we decided on the perfect plan, Plan F, only to be told by someone in the business that, yes, Plan F would be the perfect plan for you, but it is so good, it is being phased out in two years, so if you chose it, you might find yourself looking for a replacement shortly. We agreed to go with Plan G, still slightly confused and not fully sure that if we had gotten into Plan F, we would have been grandfathered in for life or not. Again, this was the downside of not having taken the time to do our research and knowing what questions to ask.

Armed with Part A (no cost) Part B ($109 a month each) Part D ($22 monthly each) and Supplemental insurance ($150 each),

I was prepared to set the budget and move forward confidently. Except for that nagging income surcharge comment. Then the bill for Part B arrived and it was five times what we had expected. What? So much for planning. And then the same happened with our Part D coverage.

Given all this intricacy, what are the right questions to ask about Medicare?

~ Which of the three plans—Original, Medicare Advantage, or Supplemental/Medigap—makes the most sense given your medical realities and your ability to afford extra charges for co-pays and deductibles?

~ What are the correct and best/required times (the enrollment period) to sign up for Medicare Part B and Part D if you are planning on using the supplemental plan? The issue may be that if you do not sign up for it in a timely fashion during the enrollment period, you may be denied the coverage you need or may be penalized financially.

~ Does your state offer the plan you want?

~ Does your insurance company of choice offer programming in your state?

~ Do you have a plan for and an understanding of the income surcharge issues you may face because of your income levels two years prior to your retirement?

~ If you are planning to purchase Part D coverage, have you compared the costs of the prescriptions you currently take that are currently charged by the different insurance companies? They may differ significantly.

~ What will you do if your circumstances change during the year?

~ If you are paying an income surcharge, what change in circumstance will lower your penalty?

~ What happens if the insurance company you work with decides not to offer coverage in your area going forward?

I remember when the *Medicare and You* workbook for all retirees arrived from the human resources department. I also recall reading it fairly carefully (skimming it) and thinking I understood what I needed to know. The problem, I have concluded, is that the people who write these summaries are not considering the diversity of the audience and are not writers; they are administrators. So, when they include a comment about "paying by Social Security discount," they glide over it in a sentence, expecting it will be covered more fully elsewhere or by someone else. Secondly, I admit that now that we have been through the crucible of having to figure this out on our own, the workbook makes a lot more sense. Clearly, it was developed by a person who knew the system so well, he or she assumed the explanations were clear. They were not so clear to us.

My other takeaway is that the system is much easier to navigate if your financial circumstances are not complicated. A very small percentage of people need to pay the income surcharge, but if you are one of them, it is an important piece of the puzzle to have in place if you are trying to get a complete assessment of your retirement budget.

My final thoughts on the Supplemental program: I have decided, in retrospect, that I did not have a nuanced view or current information on medical insurance companies, and, therefore, I may have become an insurance snob. Understandably, after nearly five decades of Blue Cross/Blue Shield—Anthem coverage (all Cadillac plans) I had a limited view of the market. Consequently, when

I called the Medicare and supplemental marketers, I was surprised to hear the names of companies I had only seen on television and billboards or read about in mailer advertisements selling insurance products. Mutual of Omaha was more familiar to me as the host of Wild Kingdom. Cigna, Aetna, Humana, and United Health Care rounded out the list. There was no Anthem, and I had wondered why? I needed to get realistic.

Then Pam joined the search with her significant sleuthing skills, and we called a number of medical providers in the area to ask which insurance company they preferred their clients/patients to subscribe to. We wanted the Gold Standard, as it were, to ensure a smooth glide path in attending to our medical needs. Surprising to us, our new medical providers really didn't seem to even understand our question.

"Do you mean what Medicare insurer do we think you should choose?" they asked.

"Well, yes, if you can," we replied.

"Then there is no answer to your question. Medicare is Medicare, and it really doesn't matter to us," they responded.

Then we dug deeper and asked to be transferred to their Human Resources offices and repeated the question. Same answer, but with a little more color commentary:

"The way Medicare works is that if you have a policy with a recognized insurance company, we have to accept it. And since all supplemental plans offer the same benefits by law, we honestly do not care which one you use, and we cannot tell you, by law, what majority of our clients use, anyway."

Welcome to this new world.

More research on the internet helped us understand that price was often the only difference and that price could vary from state to state. We also learned to ask the sales people on the phone what level of market share a company had in your state or region. We remembered that this variance is one of the consequences of having insurance regulations that do not allow medical insurance to be sold competitively across state lines. Unfortunately, it has been this way for at least the last 30 plus years. However, there is a chance that this, too, may change in the coming years.

The final news is good news. As clueless as we were about all these things, we did have a health surprise that tested the strength and resilience of our Medicare coverage, and it performed as well or better than advertised.

If I were doing this again, I would contact Medicare.gov and I would do the research to determine the name and contact information for the Medicare office in my state. Many states have programs funded by the Older Americans Act that provide free assistance with Medicare questions. While I do not have personal experience with such programs, the people I have spoken to who have availed themselves of these services assure me that what is offered will save you the trial and error process we experienced and could result in significant financial savings. One example of these programs is the SHIIP program in North Carolina.

o–¬ Key Reminders

- ~ Utilize Medicare brokers to educate yourself on choices and prices.
- ~ Align your choice of Medicare plan with your health needs—be honest and objective.
- ~ Observe and abide by Social Security and Medicare sign up times.

~ Determine through research what insurance companies operate in your state.

~ Practice comparative shopping when choosing your Medicare plans.

~ Remember that you have never been this old before, so expect to have more doctors' office visits and plan on an uptick in prescription drugs as well.

~ Pay your Medicare Part B and Part D expenses by deducting the amounts from your monthly Social Security checks to qualify for significant savings.

~ Connect with assistance programs like those created by the Older Americans Act for support in the Medicare process.

07

INSURANCE POLICIES AND COVERAGES FOR AND DURING RETIREMENT

"Don't let your tools become your process."
—Anon

There are many rules of thumb and truisms we hear and sometimes use as guideposts on our way to financial security and retirement confidence. For instance, there is an adage that you only "purchase a house to live in, not to invest in." For years people understood that purchasing or building a home was Step #1 in building a foundation for the future. Your mortgage payments served as a fail-safe way of saving for retirement because every month some of what you pay against your mortgage is a de facto payment to your retirement savings because it adds to the value of your home. When you retire, your home will probably be the foundation of your net worth.

Yet today, many young people rent or live with their parents so they can save on the costs of owning a home. Their argument is that homes are expensive: they need to be maintained; they generate tax bills; and they commit you to long-term mortgage payments in most cases. There are some who will tell you there are better ways to build equity—by paying yourself the difference between your home owner costs and your rental costs, and then investing those extra dollars. Still, after all the nuanced arguments have been made about the right strategy, it would appear that a home should primarily be bought "to live in and not to invest in."

Be assured this book has not suddenly changed direction to become a primer on housing; the example above was chosen as an analogy to make the point that you should always try to use the right tool for the right job. People can certainly make money through the appreciation in the value of their home, but there are other tools that can also be equally reliable for growing your net worth. The same is true of insurance. There are situations for which insurance is a perfect strategy and others where it is sold to people as an investment vehicle instead of as a replacement strategy for the unexpected loss of income during one's working years. In this chapter we will review some of the stories, the guidelines, the myths, and the realities and benefits of different types of insurance.

Most adages make sense, and the same can be said about insurance: think twice before you buy insurance as an investment. And yet there are many insurance people who have made a profitable living selling insurance as an investment. To explain this seeming contradiction, we need to frame the questions you need to ask about all the different types of insurance.

Life Insurance
I recall reaching the age of 60 and noticing that the content of our bulk mail had changed. I was suddenly receiving notices about

the low cost of life insurance, weekly. I was amazed that so many insurers were eager for my business. Were these people angling for years of fat premium payments or were they just seizing on a sales opportunity? The packaging was not overly subtle. For only a handful of dollars a week, I could purchase a whole life policy which would ensure that my family could (a) afford my funeral; (b) celebrate my passing with a modest inheritance; or (c) be certain that my family would be able to afford to carry on after I was gone.

At this point, maybe because my sensitivity to this trend was now heightened, I noticed the same messages being run as television ads for life insurance companies. People seemed obsessed by the opportunities represented by the aging and more vulnerable retiree market.

Insurance as Income Replacement

I was always taught that insurance is useful for one thing: replacing income. And there were two ways to do this. You could purchase a modest-sized whole life policy which would be there during your life and certainly could provide some relief in case of death; or you could purchase a relatively low-cost, term life policy which protects you only as long as you are paying the premiums, but also pays out the face amount of the policy at time of death. Term Life was tantamount to renting a whole life insurance policy. You might pay into it for 20 years and have the income replacement coverage, but you might never get any financial benefit after all those quarterly payments once you stopped paying. However, if you were to die unexpectedly while insured, you would have purchased a lot more insurance coverage than if you'd purchased a more expensive and consequently smaller dollar value, whole life policy. (Whole life is more expensive because you own the policy and are guaranteed the death benefit long after you have paid up the policy.) So, if the unimaginable were to happen and your family had to go on without you, a term life policy would probably provide more appropriate income replacement insurance for which you did not overpay.

In my lifetime, term life insurance policies became the obvious choice for those who wanted significant protection at a reasonable cost…and peace of mind. But how much replacement income would you need in order to replace your contribution to the cost of living equation in your family? Remember, you would be replacing not only your after-tax salary dollars, but also the value of your benefits—health insurance, pension payment, health savings plans, and any other support programs offered by your place of work. On top of these, you need to add in the financial commitments needed to cover the cost of your role as the on-duty parent: driving, shopping, taking the kids to that next event. Someone now needs to provide these things in your place. This calculation is complex, so insurance agents began simplifying it by telling you that you needed six times the amount of your salary. That seemed like a lot. Now, however, they suggest the right multiplier is twelve times! Frankly, this may be correct.

No one really knows because it depends on so many factors. What are your other sources of monetary relief that your family and spouse could access in response to your death? How are your family and spouse going to use the cash proceeds from the insurance? Will they use it as a long-term endowment fund, which you only spend a small percentage of annually; or as a sinking fund, which you will spend down for current expenses until it has been spent? Remember that even a half-million dollars, tax free (which it would be upon the death of the insured because it is life insurance and not salary) may not last as long as you would think. If the deceased's salary was $50,000 and you used the insurance proceeds just to replace salary, it would only last 10 years—depending on how well it had been invested. That might be enough depending on the age of your children. On the other hand, college costs alone could use up those resources for just the college tuitions of two children.

The Litany of Retirement Insurance Products

Suffice it to say that there will be plenty of people who want to get you to sign up for insurance—life insurance, income insurance (annuities), long-term care insurance, disability insurance, and dental and vision insurance preceding or in retirement. Retirees are prime targets for the insurance companies, and that's because retirees tend to be emotional about their purchases when it involves their vulnerabilities or their mortality.

One truth is that there may be a role for each of the insurances referenced in the short list above, but I would not recommend most of them as purchases when people are in the midst of their retirement. As with the tree that needed to be planted 20 years ago, there are insurances that ideally should be purchased at certain stages in your life when these coverages make the most sense and are still cost-efficient. In your early earning years, especially if you are single, but almost regardless, life insurance does not make as much sense as early investing. The dollars you are using to pay sales commissions to agents and companies and insurance premiums could be better utilized beginning tax-deferred or even after-tax savings and investment plans.

These insurances which make sense for those still working, need to be understood fully if being proposed and/or considered for purchase in preparation for or during retirement.

Disability Insurance

Disability insurance is the insurance that guarantees payments to you if you can no longer work due to injury or health issues. Usually, policy payouts are capped at 60% of salary. However, there is also a product called supplemental disability insurance which you can purchase if the 60% coverage will not meet your needs, which uses a calculation based on higher salary levels.

My experience suggests that disability insurance is one of those coverages that make sense early in one's career, and rarely is appropriate for retirees. The statistics show that a 22-year-old is 7.5 times more likely to be disabled than to die, while a 30-year-old is 4 times more likely to be disabled than to die. A 55-year-old is only 1.5 times more likely to be disabled than to die. The odds are almost 1-to-1 at age 62. So, what does that suggest?

First, it suggests that you need to know what the Social Security program offers as a benefit to those who become disabled while still working. Then you need to understand what your employer offers and whether supplemental disability coverage is available. Finally, if you are still in the workforce, you need to price out disability insurance which, you will discover, is more affordable than life insurance and may make sense in mitigating the risk of your sacrificing income because of a disabling event.

It also means that carrying disability insurance well into your golden years does not make financial sense unless a loss-of-income event would severely interfere with your retirement financial plan. The efficacy of purchasing disability insurance is one of the questions you need to add to your list. (Important note: Employer provided disability insurance payments are taxable if paid by your employer, whereas the benefits you receive in disability if you paid the premiums are not taxable because you have paid for them with after-tax dollars. You have a choice, so ask the question.)

Dental and Vision Insurance in Retirement

Pam and I had been spoiled by an employer that provided excellent vision and dental plans. Our employer-sponsored plans had covered preventative check-ups twice a year and very generous coverage for more complicated and expensive procedures. We assumed (there is that dangerous word again) there would be similar opportunities in the after-retirement insurance world. Once again, we were surprised and disappointed. When we spoke to the insurance companies we were directed to by our Medicare Insurance network, we learned the following:

~ Not all states offer the same dental programs and they insure very little of the real risk.

~ Premiums for this coverage are surprisingly high for modest coverage.

~ "You might be lucky if the State (now, your State) decides to offer a better dental coverage package next year. It certainly needs to."

~ And from the dentist offices: "You will be better off self-insuring."

Vision programs were not much different because most vision-related costs are either for routine procedures—yearly exams and lenses and frames—or for procedures too complex to insure profitably. Once again, we were back to trying to understand what our Medicare and Supplemental Plans offered in the way of support for preventative dental and eye care, and it appeared that some Medicare Plans offered basic checkups but did not have coverage for procedures like caps, root canals, or periodontics—work that was costly and not uncommon for retirees. We decided to begin to fill the old coffee tin with loose change from our trips to the store to fund our self-insurance coverage for both dental and vision costs.

The last two types of insurance we need to discuss may be helpful, but both also fit into the "better earlier than later in life" category. In the scenario where you are a decade or a decade and a half away from your retirement date, we would suggest investigating both long-term care insurance and a second-to-die life insurance policy (if you have a spouse). Both concepts benefit from placement when you are a long way from the actual need or payout.

Long-Term Care Insurance

Long-term care (LTC) insurance provides coverage for costs associated with incapacitation resulting from medical challenges. The LTC policy helps you in the case of costly medical needs relating to professional care and equipment. These policies cover short term care needs like in-home care for recuperation from a hip replacement operation; and provide coverage for costs related to more extended and serious matters like assisted living or nursing care. Most LTC policies offer inflation-protection as a rider to attenuate the risk of rising costs. Without inflation protection riders, your insured daily rates for services may be at risk for falling behind the market rates over a period of years (inflation). For example, if the policy you purchased provided coverage for $100 dollars a day of nursing home coverage, that amount of coverage might have been enough when you purchased it, but it will not be able cover the same percentage of the cost of a day of care after a decade of inflation. This means that you need to answer the question of whether to purchase inflation-protection rider or adjustment with your policy if you choose to purchase this type of coverage.

The second question you need to answer is if and then when it makes sense to purchase such a policy. LTC, when purchased during one's fifties or early sixties, provides an excellent insurance hedge against unforeseen medical situations and expenses in the future. Depending on the level of benefit you purchase and depending on the age at which you purchase it, LTC policies can be quite affordable. The earlier in your life your purchase is—within reason—the better the rate. (Note: Once again, reading the fine print and understanding all the scenarios which will be covered, before purchasing this or any insurance product, is extremely important.)

An important caveat/warning: Recently, there have been significant changes in the LTC market because many insurers severely underestimated the benefits they would be required to pay out. The industry response has been to contact policy holders and explain that they (the insurance companies) had the need and the right to change their policy terms and to charge significantly more for the continuation of the same coverage. This has forced some retirees to abandon their policies having paid into them for years and never having benefited from them.

Other LTC insurers have created a hybrid product which combines long-term care insurance with a cash value option to attract those who want the protection but may not need the care. This seems like another example of the time-honored practice of selling insurance as an investment vehicle which may carry heavy up-front costs and fees.

Both these considerations should lead you to the framing of important questions to ask a trusted insurance professional rather than a financial adviser/salesperson.

Second-to-Die Insurance

Second-to-die insurance is the other product that is certainly not for everyone, but if the parameters fit your needs, and if purchased well in advance of retirement, it can be a useful addition to one's financial and estate planning tools and strategies. The naming of this product, second-to-die insurance, unfortunately, provides a stark reminder that we all shall pass this earth at some point, so it seems both aptly and poorly named. Aside from the moniker, however, it provides a number of benefits. The policy is paid out only upon the death of the surviving partner in a couple. Because it is an insurance product, the cash benefit passes tax free to the beneficiaries (or owners of the policy) and can be used to pay estate taxes (if they still exist), pay the costs of unwinding a business, or even making resources available to provide inheritances for others or gifts to charities. Second-to-die policies may also represent a thoughtful and helpful, tax-advantaged strategy to respond to a family's special needs for continuing income and investable cash after a couples' death, especially if, for instance, a surviving dependent has ongoing, costly medical or physical needs.

Some people put their second-to-die policies in insurance trusts to keep them out of their estates, if they are concerned about taxes levied against their estates. Others use their opportunity to pass income on to their heirs through annual charitable gifting to family members to cover the premiums so they (the family members) actually own the policy and, therefore, they are eligible to receive the insurance money without estate tax or process considerations. This product can also be used for high net worth investors as a possible tax-deferred investment vehicle as long as the value of the cash in the policy does not exceed the face value of the policy. It is important to remember that all insurance is fundamentally, pure term insurance, but whole life and universal or variable life plans have savings components attached. Remember also that you pay for the additional benefit of investment potential by being assessed a higher rate (fees and commissions) than you would be paying to invest in a traditional way.

Fortunately, my time as a benefit administrator and interested participant in the retirement financial planning discussion prepared me for most of the insurance related questions. But I will list a few important questions just as reminders of certain insurance to-do's for retirees:

~ How much life insurance do you need as income replacement—during your working years and in retirement?

~ How much life insurance does your employer provide?

~ Is your employer-provided life insurance coverage portable or convertible into retirement? If yes, are the terms reasonable and sensible for you?

~ Do you have employer-provided disability insurance?

~ What percentage of your income does your disability insurance cover?

- Do you need supplemental disability insurance–either from your employer, if available, or from a private company?

- What will Social Security provide if you are disabled while working? And for how long will you receive this disability benefit?

- How does your disability plan integrate with the Social Security benefit?

- How will you cover the "elimination" period (time between your disability and your first disability payment) of disability insurance before you begin to receive benefits?

- Should a form of life insurance (whole life, variable rate, straight term, or second-to-die) be a part of your retirement portfolio?

- Why do/would you need life insurance at this stage of your life, and what role will it play in your retirement planning?

- Are you using life insurance as an income replacement vehicle or as an investment vehicle?

- What is the cost/benefit analysis of purchasing Long-term care (LTC) insurance?

- What is the cost/benefit rationale for purchasing dental or vision insurance in retirement? (There may be a rationale to do so in your situation.)

I will skip over the highly controversial annuity question until later. Given that people often explain annuities as something that is sold and not usually bought, consider yourself warned. Most people believe that annuities are the time-share deals of the financial industry. Many people own them, did not fully understand them when they purchased them, and cannot get rid of them when the annual charges add up while the benefits diminish.

Annuities may have a place in the portfolios of some people, but they should only be considered when there is a need for a guaranteed income source.

This discussion of insurances should take us back to the Five Ws—Why, Who, When, Where, and What. Why is insurance the right approach to solving a certain problem or accessing an opportunity? Who needs to be insured and for how much? When should you purchase the product you choose? Where or from whom should you purchase it? And finally, what should you purchase? Then educate yourself about the insurance market and its products or speak with a person you can trust who knows the insurance space. "Measure twice and cut once."

o⚊ Key Reminders

~ Use the right tool for the right job, i.e. use insurance for covering risk and not for investing.

~ Just as it is true for investments, fees and commissions matter when considering and purchasing insurance products.

~ Always read the fine print on any insurance contract to ensure the cost/benefit analysis works in your situation and to make certain you understand what you are signing up for.

~ Make sure you buy what you need and ask for rather than buying what people are trying to sell you.

08

SOCIAL SECURITY: TIMING? OPTIONS? SECURITY?

"Let our advance worrying become our advance thinking and planning."
—Winston Churchill

We now need to review the options for retirees to determine the amount of the Social Security income they will receive monthly to ensure that distribution meets expectations. Everyone advising you personally or through infomercials will have an opinion about when a retiree or retired couple should begin to draw Social Security. If you need the monthly income from Social Security as soon as you qualify for benefits, you should draw when you have the need. If you have saved other taxable income for retirement or can manage your financial obligations without your monthly government check, you should factor in this as part of your cost/benefit analysis.

You might be asking how you can control or determine what your Social Security payment will be when you have been told for years through your Social Security benefit updates approximately how much of a benefit you will receive when you retire. The reality is that for every year you delay taking your Social Security payments after your normal retirement age, you will get an 8% annual increase in the value of your Social Security benefit. Therefore, you definitely need to weigh the relative benefit of waiting a year to receive your benefits and having the payout value of your benefit increase by 8% over the payout you would be getting if you began taking your benefit at your normal retirement age, or if you took your benefit at your normal retirement age and attempted to earn that same 8% annually by investing your Social Security check in other investments. And I assure you getting an 8% return is no easy task. One benefit in this analysis, therefore, may be getting the money you need now by turning on the cash flow process; whereas, the cost would be forgoing a guaranteed 8% return for your annual benefit for the rest of your life. Clearly, the most important consideration is need and, therefore, timing. When do you really and truly need the money?

Some people may opt to begin Social Security benefits at age 62 because it is allowed by law and/or because they need the money as soon as possible. By taking the benefit early, you will only be receiving 80% of the full retirement amount that you would have received at your normal retirement age. Others may decide to take the money early because they do not need these Social Security dollars to live on and would just as soon begin getting paid back for all those years of contributing to a program they didn't fully understand, so they could begin investing that money at the earliest possible time. There is also a case to be made if a retiree has serious health issues and worries about not living long enough to get the life-long investment of hard-earned dollars back. My point is that there are good and not-so-good reasons for choosing to withdraw early, and you need to think hard about the cost/benefit analysis and timing in making this important decision. This is another area potential retirees need to understand well before deciding, so it needs to be added to the list of questions and research topics all retirees need to consider.

Remember that the questions single people have will be very different from the questions couples should be asking. Couples have options for a spouse benefiting from his or her spouse's pay-outs after the death of the spouse. Furthermore, divorced spouses have opportunities for assuming a divorced spouse's benefits before and after the death of the divorced spouse.

In our case there was no question to be answered. We had decided that our retirement age was going to be age 70, and there would be no additional 8% annual benefit available by waiting to claim our Social Security benefits after age 70. As a matter of fact, there is no financial benefit to waiting to draw beyond age 70 ever. If you are not going to draw at age 70 for any reason, that would be tantamount to declining benefits. In our case by waiting until age 70, we had increased our annual benefit amount by the full 8% a year for the four years beyond our normal retirement age of 65. If we had taken the money at 65 and invested it for those five years, we would probably not have earned as much as the 8% annual increase since we would have been cautious investors trying to protect the money in anticipation of retirement. Furthermore, we would have been paying taxes on those benefits every year because we were still employed and receiving a salary. This meant that our Social Security dollars were growing tax-deferred for those four years. Additionally, we were guaranteed the 8% increase per annum, and as most of us know, there are few guaranteed returns when investing.

People from the radio talk show/commercials for financial planning, the contributors to AARP, and financial planners all have their advice on when is the best time to draw your Social Security. Again, everyone's circumstances are different, and all these circumstances affect each person's cost/benefit analysis. Health, family longevity history, financial planning milestones, marital status, an unforeseen need—all these situations and circumstances can and should be factored into your decision-making. Again, asking the right questions matters.

Regardless of your decision on when to draw, you must dutifully sign up at your Social Security office during the sign-up period—which spans six months—three months before you turn age 65 until three months after that date, regardless of whether you plan to draw when eligible for benefits. You are not turning on the flow of Social Security checks when you sign up at age 65; your monthly income benefits will begin only after you have informed Social Security of your start date. You also need to understand this is a clearly delineated enrollment period for signing up with Social Security administration for Medicare; and you do not want to be the person who misses that window. This sign up time period is your enrollment opportunity for Medicare Part A and Part B; but as clearly advertised as this sign up guidance is, the entire process can be slightly confusing.

Harkening back to our *Leave It To Beaver* comparison, when the Social Security administration was put into place over sixty years ago, most people retired at the "required" retirement age. Back then workers were not allowed to choose to work longer on their own volition. The government and, by extension, their employers literally had the power to force people to retire at age 65. Therefore, the normal retirement age and the required retirement age were the same. Today that is not the case. Most baby-boomers, who are retiring in droves today, have been assigned a normal retirement age which is greater than 65. My normal retirement date was 65 and 6 months. Pam's age qualification was 66 years and 2 months. So, when you sign up (and you *really* must do so) three months before your 65th birthday and get your automatic enrollment in Medicare Part A completed, you may still be working, might still be on an employer's medical plan, and may still not be benefiting from or paying for Medicare.

One note of importance and potential confusion is worth mentioning. When you sign up for Social Security and are automatically enrolled in Medicare Part A, you do not need to enroll in Part B if you are still on your employer's medical plan. However, if you will not continue on your employer's plan, and you do not take this opportunity to enroll in Medicare Part B—which is essential—you may be penalized financially for not meeting the sign-up guidelines for Medicare Part B during the initial enrollment period.

This is not rocket science, but it can be confusing if you are planning to work beyond age 66 or 67—or past whatever your normal retirement age and benefit eligible ages are. This was the case for both Pam and me. We signed up three months prior to our 65th birthdays and were automatically enrolled in Medicare Part A. We did not enroll in Part B at that time because we were still on our employer-sponsored medical plan and would be for four more years. We had read all the warnings about penalties for not signing up for Part B at the proper time, but we felt secure in knowing that we were covered by employer-provided medical coverage until we retired and left our employer-sponsored plan.

Then, nearly a year after our retirement, and much to our surprise, we received an official letter in the mail from the Social Security administration suggesting officiously that we were going to be assessed a penalty because we had not signed up in a timely fashion for our Part B coverage. Even for someone like me who had been decoding serious, business letters my entire career, this missive was certainly misleading, inappropriate, and alarming. My first thought was what would a senior citizen make of this? Then I remembered I was one of those. That only made me more angry. I could just see some elderly person being totally flummoxed and trying to figure out where the extra penalty money would come from. As it turned out, we were not going to be penalized, but someone wanted us to be very clear that if we could not prove we had stayed on our employer's plan, we would be paying a penalty.

This was our first indication of how poorly the Social Security administration communicates with its customers in writing; and now after being on Social Security for more than a year, I would double down on the complaint. I have no complaints, however, about their oral communication. In fact, once you get them on the phone, they are most helpful and absolutely clear. So, with the caveat that the waiting time for a call to be answered can be legendary, we determined that calling your Social Security office is worth the wait. To lessen the waiting anxiety, we learned to choose the option of a call back at an appointed time the answering system offered in lieu of holding on the line for an eternity. They were very good about keeping to these scheduled call-backs, and they were committed once on the call to getting you the information that you requested, and, more importantly, that you needed.

The only other point about this process you need to be aware of is that Social Security's billing system also leaves something to be desired. As an example, one day we received a bill for an amount of money that absolutely made no sense to us. The numbers just didn't tie together with any combination of fees or charges we had expected. As a former CFO I considered this to be a bright line in the sand for me; I needed to be able to understand what I was paying for before writing a check, so I called. When I demanded an explanation, a very nice customer-service representative explained to me that they had thrown together four separate billing amounts which represented four different types of charges and simply lumped them together. I asked as pleasantly as I could how would I ever have known what I was paying for and whether the charges were accurate. She responded immediately, "You wouldn't, but we would; and our records are the ones that matter."

Social Security may be frustrating at times because it represents and operates like a huge, bureaucratic machine, but the people who work there mean well, have more pressing concerns than my or your equanimity, and they are dealing with the safety, security, and well-being of millions of people who represent a diversity of needs and challenges I could never imagine.

A few reminders:

- Social Security and Medicare—Original and Medicare Part C (Advantage)—are closely linked.
- Social Security has nothing to do with any Supplemental/ Medigap program. Supplemental contracts are created by private insurance companies, and they are not part of the government's entitlement program.
- Social Security checks arrive at your bank or to your home approximately a month after you qualify. If your birthday is in early September, you can plan to receive your Social Security check in early October—not on or within a few

days or weeks of your birthday. That is the way the system works, so you need to plan for that timing.

~ The amount of tax you pay for your Social Security depends on the amount of income you earn or have earned in the two years before you retire. If you earn at or above the highest income level they classify, 50% to 85% of your benefit will be taxed at your regular rate.

~ Medicaid is a combination state and federal medical care option/program that allows people with financial challenges to apply for services. (Note: I will not be covering this program since I have had no direct experience with it and my knowledge is mostly hearsay and second hand. I can assure you, however, that locating information at Medicaid.gov will provide valuable information.)

~ Under the current system you have the right and the opportunity to change your Medicare coverages—during every enrollment period, which usually lasts from mid-October until early or mid-December—to accommodate any changes in your health care needs or to check prices for a more competitive rate and less expensive coverage for the coming year.

~ Your Social Security income is intended to serve as a base for your retirement savings. Some financial planners use the figure of 25% to 50% of your retirement income coming from Social Security, with the remainder coming from your 403(b)s, 401(k)s, IRAs, and personal savings programs and accounts. This is simply a guideline and not a hard and fast rule.

~ Survivor benefits for the deceased spouse or for any child under age 18 include the ability to exchange a spouse's current SS benefits for those of the deceased spouse, if they are higher. In addition, there will be a lump sum death benefit (modest amount).

~ Social Security is fairly straight forward and only becomes complicated in the interface with Medicare and the IRS.

The best news is that the internet, hundreds of paid commercials, financial planners, and friends will have more than enough information as long as you ask the right questions and follow your plan. So, a quick drill you should run:

~ Who qualifies for Social Security?

~ Who in your family should activate the benefit stream first (couples)?

~ Why? How does this fit the strategy and value proposition?

~ What are you eligible for in terms of benefits? How do you know?

~ When do you qualify?

~ When do you need to sign up for Social Security and Medicare? (Enrollment period.)

~ When should you and/or your spouse take your benefits?

Lastly, there has been much discussion and disruptive dialogue about the viability and security of Social Security going forward. There is a good explanation for this. The dollars that were deducted from your pay checks all those years and the money paid in by your employer is not your money. It goes into a huge fund with payroll taxes and other payments to the government to pay for Social Security and other entitlements. This is the perfect example of the saying that money is fungible. Its fungibility means it can be used for a variety of purposes; therefore, as long as the taxes keep flowing into this giant catch-all fund, there will be money for benefits. The more probable questions for future retirees might very well be about age requirements and the rate of return for delaying your benefits. I expect that Social Security in a familiar form will still be available 15 years from now. My only caution would be that you still need to plan for all eventualities and pull up the socialsecurity.gov website regularly to stay informed.

⌐ Key Reminders

~ Cost benefit analysis, timing, and cash flow analysis are key variables in the question about when to take your Social Security benefits.

~ Remember, you have some control over the amount of your benefit you receive by adjusting the timing of turning on your benefit.

~ Social Security is an important and foundational piece of your retirement cash flow puzzle.

~ Always observe and adhere to enrollment period deadlines and windows for both Social Security and Medicare.

~ Your Social Security administration office is a good source of information for you in retirement.

09

INVESTMENTS AND INVESTING: QUESTIONS AND CONCERNS YOU NEED TO UNDERSTAND

"Price is what you pay. Value is what you get."
—Warren Buffett

I would ask you to recall the example of the radio salesman/financial planner/estate guru who was promoting his two most important rules of retirement: Rule #1—Just don't lose the money; and Rule #2—Remember Rule #1. Remember also that this quote should be attributed to The Oracle of Omaha, Warren Buffett. So now we can move on to the preservation of principle.

This premise is one shared by many people, but it has an interesting history. Before individual IRAs came into play for the average wage earner, and before there were readily accessible mutual funds, and long before there were passive investments, i.e. index funds that are not actively managed by a broker (until the late 1960s or early '70s), employers put their employee pension or their retirement dollars into a fund to purchase company stock or to be invested in some combination of stocks and bonds. The employer had virtually no contractual responsibility to generate safe and reasonable returns or even reasonable fees for investment products. In return the employee received a guaranteed benefit (amount) based on the employee's length of service and a percentage of pay, or the employee received a payment based on what was generated by growth in the company stock. This was, at best, a good faith and best effort environment. Then Peter Lynch of the Magellan Fund at Fidelity and Jack Bogle at Vanguard exploded onto the scene, and the investment, retirement and pension worlds changed dramatically.

I will not rehearse all these changes but suffice it to say that as the years passed, employers and employees both had to take on greater responsibility for their financial well-being in the retirement fund process. When I was a CFO, I recall people coming to me saying they had been counseled years earlier when they were eligible to participate in the retirement plan, to put half their retirement money into bonds (fixed income) and half into stocks (equities); and now they were wondering what would have happened to their funds if they had used a 75% equity and 25% bond ratio for their investments, or a 100% equity commitment. I researched the market results for the period and found the results fascinating; but they did not bring any miraculous clarity to the discussion.

First, the returns on fixed income in the 1970s and early '80s were quite impressive, while returns on equities during those years were modest. Conversely, returns for equities from 1985–2000 were impressive and mostly consistent, and bond returns, while less strong, were reasonably rewarding as well. Still, those who had bet more on equities than on fixed income had gained more for their retirements during almost any ten-year period. One individual I spoke with asked me to compare the results of a 100% fixed income allocation for his pension investments from 1985 to 1995 with what the results might have been if he had made a 100% commitment to equities in the same time period for his portfolio. I will caution you that the results of this exercise should not be considered anything more than informal research, but I determined that a $10,000 investment in a fixed income, index fund generated 33% less than the same amount invested in an equities fund for that ten-year period. During those years, equities were on a bull market run. I then asked him why he'd chosen the fixed income strategy. His response surprised me. He said he really didn't know the difference between equities and bonds, except that he'd heard that bonds were safe and without risk, while investing in the stock market was more like gambling. Wow. Conceptually interesting, but not a fair representation of these different approaches.

I learned very early on as a fiduciary for an endowment fund for a school that, in general and going back as far as World War II, equities have on average outperformed fixed incomes, with equities averaging 6% per annum and bonds producing a 4% return annually. I was also taught that an easy if somewhat simplistic way of thinking about the differences between equities and fixed income instruments was to categorize equities as investments in profit-making, while fixed incomes were generally investments in debt. I created the following example to help explain the difference:

You have $1,000 to invest, and you have two choices: (1) to purchase a piece of a business you want to invest in and become a part owner in it, or (2) to lend your money to the owner of that business so he can invest in it, in return for an agreed upon interest payment for the term of the lending agreement. In choice #1, as a part owner of the business, if the business generates profits, you as a shareholder also profit. As the value of the business goes up, your share is worth more.

If, on the other hand, you determine you do not want to bet on the ability of the business owner to generate growth and profits, you can decide to lend your money to the owner at an agreed upon rate for an agreed upon length of time. ($1,000 loaned in return for a 5% return annually for five years.) And so long as the business stays afloat, and the cash flow is as predicted, you get the 5% return every pay period for the term of the agreement. That is why people like investing in debt. It is more predictable and seems less risky.

Similarly, if the business you have ownership in grows in market share and value, your $1,000 investment will be worth more by the same percentage the business has grown. The company's growth is not guaranteed, so ownership, or what I call investing in profit-making, is indeed riskier than the mostly guaranteed return on debt. However, there are really no guarantees, and there are no iron-clad assurances in either approach, but over time, profit historically has and should in the future generally outperform debt. That was a truthful answer, but it was not the answer to the right question.

Risk Tolerance

This explanation has always helped me understand why it was so important to understand your own risk tolerance profile. If you are comfortable with more risk in your investment portfolio and your life, and if you can still sleep at night knowing you are betting on the growth of a company you are not running, then a greater percentage of equities in your retirement portfolio makes sense for you. However, if you are haunted by the stories of the Great Depression of the late '20s, the market meltdown of 1987, the bursting of the Tech Bubble in 2000, the no-market-gain years from 2001-2004, or the Great Recession in 2008, you will have to think hard about your appetite for risk. That is when you need to look at investment horizons—how long you have before you need the money—and the types of equities if any, in which you might invest.

The key point for the purpose of this primer is to ensure that you understand both what you are investing in as well as the relative volatility as well as the risk (two different concepts) of the different approaches to investing. Yes, everything comes with risk, so first you need to understand that reality. You also need to know that as you think about the 20 to 25 years you will have in retirement, you will need to factor in the probability that generating a very modest return, say one produced by a guaranteed, low risk portfolio of fixed income investments, might not ensure that you will be able to preserve your buying power, probably because of inflation. This reality should then prompt more discussion about how to preserve your buying power by growing your portfolio; so, you may need to give some additional consideration to investing in equities and developing a more diversified approach to your asset allocation.

People first jumped on the pendulum swing of more equity growth from their portfolios, regardless of their situation, because they realized they needed 6%-8% annual returns to preserve their buying power for the three decades they needed to fund from their retirement portfolio. Now, the pendulum has swung back to more balance in one's portfolio since the Tech Bubble burst and the Recession of 2008 happened. People approaching or entering retirement are now considering more thoughtful and nuanced ways to position their savings and retirement plans for both safety and growth. Remember that every retiree situation is a little or even very different, and while some people can and should take on more risk, others need to save their way to security because they are risk averse.

It seems that this sea change in investing may have led to a new obsession: How am I going to replace my paycheck in retirement? Maybe this is the new number question. Let's begin to do the math:

Income Sources

~ You should know for certain what your Social Security income after taxes and minus charges for Medicare will be because you have already considered the cost/benefit and the timing of your choice of when to take those benefits and what Medicare program you will select.

~ You also know, if applicable, what your spouse's Social Security income minus Medicare charges and taxes will be. Those are the first two checks in the mail you can count on.

~ Then there is your retirement plan income. Depending on your age when you retire and when you start receiving income, you are not required to withdraw any specified amount until after you have reached the age of seventy and a half. That does not mean you cannot take money from this fund earlier; rather, you are just not obligated to do so. That tax-deferred money will only be taxed when you take it from your plan as a distribution as regular income, so the number you should be looking at is net income, a.k.a. cash flow.

~ Next is to identify any other IRA income you might have access to. Once again you need to answer the timing and cost/benefit questions, since this money can continue to grow tax-deferred until age 70½, when you'll need to withdraw the percentage of your IRA total dollars you are required to take out of your retirement account.

~ The requirement for withdrawal is called an RMD, a required minimum distribution.

~ Another source may be your taxable savings and investments. These are very important since they can be drawn on without incurring taxes on the base amount; only on what you earned on the savings or investments. (Note: These taxable investment accounts actually play an important role in a retirement portfolio, and that is why I always recommend putting some of your financial eggs in the personal investments, taxable basket and not automatically over-funding your tax deferred accounts, especially if you have enough resources to make a choice and can actually do both.)

Annuities

The final topic on this aspect of your retirement, your cash flow analysis, is insured contracts. The technical term used in the financial insurance space—like TIAA or Vanguard—is annuity contract. I eviscerated the traditional annuity product earlier in this primer, but I need to double back and explain that there are annuities to avoid and then there are annuities that might be useful or appropriate.

In taking on this topic I am once again a little out of my depth because I am not an expert on the subject. I will tell you that one of the most successful financial planners in our area has a commercial suggesting that investors looking for advice come to him because he will "never sell you an annuity…no way in hell!"

However, I have done enough research on annuities to know that there are important questions to ask before deciding whether an annuity is right for you. In the simplest terms the annuity strategy involves exchanging an amount of your hard-earned money—at a point in time—for a guaranteed stream of income, over a guaranteed period of time, now or in the future. That's the best news. The worst news is that, as is true with most insurance products, you will pay significant fees and commissions to purchase and service the contract, in exchange for the income stream. This means that looking at annuities should trigger the cost/benefit analysis I have hammered home to you to convince you that this is not for you; it's too expensive and too risky. Unless...unless, your personal, family, or financial situation either requires or allows you to create a guaranteed income stream from an annuity that makes sense.

There are two main types of annuities that are available. The first is a tax-deferred annuity, and the second is an income annuity. With a tax-deferred annuity, you purchase a contract that you pay for well in advance. Then your contribution(s) grows tax-deferred over time awaiting the start of the income stream, possibly when you retire. This sounds like a plausible concept, and it would be if not for the fee and commission structure and for the byzantine details and loop holes of its architecture. It would be tantamount to paying a 7% upfront fee on an indexed, no-load mutual fund.

The second type is really the only annuity product worth considering seriously, and then only if there is a specific need for an additional, guaranteed income stream. This product is much closer to what TIAA has offered to its retiree clients for years. The TIAA fees are lower, but there are also fees associated with the guaranteed part of the commitment. The non-TIAA product operates as follows: You purchase a contract from the insurer who holds and invests the funds you provide and, in return, provides a guaranteed income stream for a guaranteed period, i.e. 10 or 20 years. There are additional agreements in the contract, such as limits on the amount of growth you can receive on the investment dollars you put in to create the annuity, or how much loss of value you can suffer on these investments; but in essence the annuitant (you) is assured a steady stream of income for the period of the contract and beyond, if you live beyond that timeframe. But remember, there are still the fees and commissions you pay for the product, so this security may come at a high cost. That's why I caution anyone to measure twice before you cut once (make the decision) before buying insurance for investment purposes.

Regardless of the above cautions, there may be a place for this income strategy for someone who has more limited resources for retirement and may not be able to depend on investment income to supplement other retirement savings. Since there are no more salary checks in the mail in retirement, retirees need to replace at least some of that pre-retirement income. A financial advisor I trust once asked me if I had considered annuities for a part of our retirement funding plan. I recoiled in horror. "Oh, one of those, are you?" I thought. "A fee hound?" I thought. But he continued his reasoning thoughtfully. He explained that regardless of an individual's financial situation, it was helpful, even comforting, to have a few checks in the mail coming on a predictable schedule, as it were. We all need to know, he continued, that our money is working for us and that there could be an additional stream of income we could depend on. I declined his offer, but I learned from his advice.

That scenario and its explanation got me thinking: Maybe boredom was less of a factor in the numbers of retirees failing retirement than financial insecurity and financial fear. If you have been the breadwinner or one of them, you may find the transition to retirement too much of a guilt trip for you to accept. Remember, if there is no number to attain and because it is difficult to generate checks for the mailbox, retiring can feel like walking on a slippery slope. That can make people do surprising things.

I do feel the need to put in a good word for the annuitized payouts TIAA or Vanguard or other reputable financial firms offer. Depending on the vintage of your investments—that is, when you or your employer invested them—you might be surprised to discover how generous a percentage return they guarantee for your lifetime. Yes, there are fees, but they are worth considering. The downside may be that you can end up having nothing left for dependents, but for those who need to or can afford to do it, it may prove to be responsive to a number of your needs.

I also want to highlight a warning, or at least provide the information, that when you sign up for a beneficiary/spousal benefit of 50% or 100% as part of your pension or annuity choice, you are effectively buying an insurance policy on your investment with all the costs and limitations of insurance policies. You really need to think this decision through before you and your spouse sign on the dotted line. This can be an expensive decision unless there are specific reasons for using this strategy. This analysis cuts both ways, however. I knew a couple, one of whom, the wife, had struggled with her health. Her husband was rarely ever ill. When they signed up for his pension, they both believed that the wife would pass first, so he did not sign up for the spousal benefit but took 100% for himself. Almost immediately upon retirement, he died of a heart attack, and she was left with no income stream from his pension. There is risk in every decision.

All that said, there are no right answers to the questions about how to invest and what to invest in. The only thing you can do is try to find someone you trust and then educate yourself about what that advisor is suggesting for you. As former President Reagan famously suggested, "Trust, and then verify."

In closing this chapter, I want to remind you of the variety of risks you will have to learn to manage in retirement. This list may not be exhaustive, but it is complete enough to be daunting and I hope it provides a good start. But first a caution. You need to understand that risk and volatility are often used interchangeably and usually incorrectly. They are not the same thing. Without giving you too arcane an explanation, the simple difference is captured in considering the risk involved in an investment in equities as being relatively low as shown by the analysis of the performance of a diversified, low-fee index fund over fifty years when compared to a similar commitment to government securities, like treasury bills, over the same time period. The objective comparison may surprise you, but that is because you may be equating risk with volatility. That same stock portfolio is not risky because we know that stocks outperform fixed incomes over time. However, that same portfolio of stocks probably and usually will have more volatility—swings in price and value—because the price of equity positions can shift hourly, daily, weekly and monthly; while the return on the bonds rarely changes. So, there is less risk in your getting a better return over time in equities, but there will be more volatility (abrupt changes in value) in that same commitment.

Just recall Buffett's warning about risk which is "never test the depth of the river with both feet."

⚭ Key Reminders

- ～ Stocks have generally outperformed bonds since financial records have been kept.
- ～ Equities are investments in profit; bonds are investments in debt.
- ～ Know your risk-tolerance profile before making investment decisions in retirement—peace of mind matters.
- ～ Risk is not the same as volatility.
- ～ Make certain you understand your sources of income.
- ～ Remember that annuities are most often sold to you.
- ～ Read the fine print on any retirement-related contract.
- ～ Do not invest in anything you do not understand.
- ～ Seek investment, insurance, or estate planning help if you need it…and you probably do.

10

UNDERSTANDING AND CONTROLLING RISK
AND VOLATILITY

*"In the short run, the market is a voting
machine, and in the long run, it's a
weighing machine."*
—Benjamin Gordon

I want to take a few minutes in this chapter to discuss the somewhat arcane topic I introduced in the last chapter: Risk. We hear
about risk in connection to stocks all the time; and as I pointed
out in the last chapter, people often conflate the concepts of risk
and volatility. They are not the same because one refers to behavior
(volatility) while the other refers to inherent safety (risk). Things
that are volatile are not necessarily risky. They are not necessarily consistent and dependable, so they may be risky in the short
term; but they could tend to smooth out over longer periods of
time—like the stock market over the last 75 years during which
time it averaged 6% a year. Recently, a financial commentator and
analyst was reminding investors watching her show that when the
Market corrects—retrenches by giving up some of the gains it has
made over time—investors have a choice: take the riskier course

by getting back into the Market or the safer course of action by investing in treasuries or bonds. I would have preferred that she explain with a more nuanced approach. People may be accepting or taking on more volatility risk when they invest in stocks, but nearly all investments have inherent risk. The term "risk" is not only used when talking about the uncertainty of markets; it is also used when referring to the types of risk there are that relate to all investments. These kinds of risk are not generic; rather, they are specific to actions or realities in the markets (bonds or equities) and they influence the safety or risk associated with an investment. We often hear about the risk of inflation or the risk associated with the direction of interest rates. These types of risk have an impact on the Markets, so you will need to have at least a basic understanding of the different types of risk there are that will influence your outcomes as an investor, so you can at least ask the right questions.

Interest Rate Risk

We hear often about the financial markets having the jitters about what the Federal Reserve (Fed) will do about interest rates. Interest rate risk is certainly important, especially since the Recession of 2008. One of the strategies for helping the economy recover from that debacle was to control the interest rate environment. Quantitative easing (QE) appeared in every article on financial risk. Quantitative Easing is when the Fed buys up predetermined securities to increase the money supply while depressing interest rates. Once the Fed started doing this to quell the damage from the 2008 meltdown, the question persisted how long QE would continue. Would the Fed allow rates to go up naturally? Would the Fed continue to depress rates artificially and keep them at an unprecedented, low level? Regardless of the answers to these important questions, interest rate hikes or rate depression can impact one's retirement plan. Some of you will remember the nearly crippling inflation and deflation of the 1970s. Interest rate fluctuation does matter to the markets and, therefore, should matter to retirees. Note: Most of the precipitous drops in the stock market since the end of 2017 were the result of concern over interest rate risk—interest rates rising too quickly with a little political and free-trade risk mixed in.

You need to remember that when interest rates rise, the bonds you purchased in a lower interest rate environment now have less underlying value than before interest rates went up. This uptick in the rates of return on any new bonds on the market consequently depresses the price a buyer is willing to pay for your older bonds, since the buyer can now purchase new bonds with a higher paying coupon or interest rate. Interest rates or, using the example of what people are willing to pay you to borrow your money, are now higher. That's why people say somewhat simplistically that bonds go down when interest rates rise. There is a key idea to keep in mind if you are holding bonds in a rising rate environment: while they may be less saleable, they will still pay the same interest you were getting before the interest rates rose. The interest that the bonds in your portfolio pay to you will not change on interest rate increases; only the underlying value of the bond—what someone is willing to pay you for it if you chose to sell it at that time—is impacted.

That means that if you are forced to sell bond positions in a rising interest rate environment, you will probably reap less than you sowed and de facto will lose money. So, yes, interest rate movement represents a risk for retirees that keeps people up at night, reminding us, importantly, that even bonds and other fixed income vehicles have volatility attached to them. The key is not to sell bonds if you can avoid it on those upward interest rate adjustments. Similarly, when interest rates go down, the underlying value of your bond portfolio increases, triggering at least the question of whether a sale makes sense. (Note: There is good news when rates go up—banks adjust upward what they are willing to pay in savings and money market accounts. Remember the days when you could get 5% from a savings account?)

Market Risk

Capital preservation—not losing the money—may be an extremely important reminder for all retirees, so any stock and/or bond losses in value represent real losses for those depending on positive returns. The reason to invest is to grow the value of your investments, not to lose it. Imagine those retiring in 2008 when the market dropped between 39% and 50%, depending on their investment strategy. That is why many people are timid at best and terrified at worst to risk their money in the markets unless there are guaranteed returns, which, as we now know, there are not. This leads us back to the importance of developing an investor's risk tolerance profile to determine how much risk, if any, is appropriate for you in retirement. There are those who get nervous with anything riskier than cash, and those who are willing to bet it all on a market that often delivers.

Currency Risk

Currency risk is far more subtle, but the strength of the dollar against other world currencies does matter. When the dollar is worth more vis a vis the Euro or the Yen, it has an impact on trade numbers. Generally, a weaker dollar is good for the equity market because exported goods are cheaper and we export more, satisfying the need of the Market for good export numbers which support businesses…reference what was happening in 2017–2018 with a relatively weaker dollar in '17, but a strengthening dollar in '18. This analysis is not something most investors worry about, but it is an interesting data point to be able to reference as you watch for signs of change in the marketplace.

Liquidity Risk

A far less obvious but still important risk is liquidity risk. Liquidity risk is the risk associated with the amount of time it takes you to move out of a position you have in the market. Say, for instance, you see the market tanking and want to flee to the safety of cash. How long will it take you to cash out? As a longtime, endowment fiduciary and observer, I understand well that there are significant risks in lack of liquidity. Many investors who thought they had liquid investment accounts learned a tough lesson in 2008 about how little liquidity there actually is when mechanized/automatic trading programs can move into and out of markets before individual investors in a mutual fund or with some modest stock positions can even think about converting their investment into cash. The mass selling of securities can happen too fast for anyone to be assured of true liquidity, but investors should be aware of how much relative liquidity they have in their portfolios. How quickly can you liquidate a position in a fund or a stock is one of the helpful questions you need to know the answer to. (I can assure you it is not minutes or even hours. It may be days.) This risk simply provides another data point for you to evaluate both your investment and the person recommending the investment to you.

Inflation Risk

Then there is inflation risk which is probably the most insidious of all types of risk. It is the number one threat to a retiree's being successful with his, her, or their financial plan for retirement. Inflation determines how much your dollar can purchase, so if five years into retirement your dollar can only buy 80% of what you were able to buy when you retired, you either need to buy less or generate more money for expenses. Inflation is tied to the Federal Reserve and its monetary policy, to business development, to debt, and to economic growth. You do not need to understand all the levers of inflation, but you do need to keep an eye on the relative purchasing power of your money over time and be fluid about responding to changes that negatively affect your financial plan. The CPI (Consumer Price Index) is the index used to track inflation, but the CPI calculation does not include all expenses that retirees will have. It does not take into consideration the cost of operating your car or heating your home, but it is a helpful indicator. It also is the number which will determine how much your Social Security will be adjusted on an annual basis.

That means that unless you are a professional who has earned his or her reputation over many financial cycles, you have very little chance of understanding all this complexity. Even after 32 years sitting on finance and investment committees listening to some of the most revered financial analysts and stock pickers or market-trend followers, I cannot do my own investing. I am able, however, to decide how much risk I can tolerate or afford. I can also understand and then decide whether bonds or equity funds make the most sense for me.

Fee Risk

Maybe most important for people reading this primer is the reminder that fees matter. You need to know what you are paying for investment advice or for the costs of trading. You need to understand if there are commissions, front-end loaded fees, and any charges for other services you are paying. What you pay in fees ultimately comes out of your return on your investment. However, I also understand that it is total return that counts in the end. If I can get investment advice for 1% and generate a 6% to 8% return, I am better off than investing on my own and generating 3% to 5%. Total return matters as well as fees, but *fees matter.*

Tax Risk

Finally, and maybe most important, I have learned to select investment strategies that are tax efficient. For example, if income projections for the year put Pam and me on the bubble of a higher tax bracket, we are going to think seriously about the tax-free nature of municipal bonds for our next investment. We also understand that if we are receiving dividends and interest from a taxable portfolio that we have created over the years, we might be smart to take the taxable returns before we harvest tax-deferred monies; once again for tax efficiency. Now that we are in retirement and are learning to control our required minimum distribution income from our IRAs and 403(b)s, our tax considerations and strategies or tactics have begun to influence the way we invest and the way we draw income from our investments. For instance, we have decided to use our RMDs to fund our annual, charitable giving, since by electing to send RMD distributions directly to charities, we will avoid paying taxes on those RMD monies.

There are a number of brokerage services we pay attention to that provide generic advice for retirees on replacing your paycheck. The general principles they recommend are extremely sensible, and a list I have put together from their recommendations will provide helpful closure to what we have been discussing in this chapter and earlier ones. Their aggregated guidance is as follows:

~ Calculate your net worth and the amount of resources you will bring into retirement.

~ Determine your goals for retirement—that mission statement and your goals and objectives—and your value proposition for retirement.

~ Decide what you'll need to live on—predictable expenses.

~ Determine expenses for needs and goals.

~ Monitor inflation risk and determine longevity risk.

~ Get advice on how to structure your account to produce the growth and income you expect to need.

~ Decide how much market risk you are willing to assume.

~ Plan for the unexpected.

~ If possible do not draw more than 4% of your investments' value annually as a way of keeping pace with inflation.

~ Balance your needs for both income and growth and do not underestimate the need for growth.

~ Manage your taxes.

~ Stay fluid and be flexible in your investment strategies and planning—knowing that things may change.

The recommendations above make sense and duplicate nicely what we have already outlined. I think it is true that just about anyone in the financial business you talk to will provide the same advice. If any advisor is trying to take you in a different direction, you definitely need a second opinion.

At the end of the day actually knowing what to do is easier than having the discipline to follow the plan and actually to do what you committed to doing. Remember Peter Drucker's warning about "culture eating strategy for breakfast every time." The wrong spending culture can devour the best laid savings and retirement plans.

Just as I was rereading this chapter about the replacement of income, I took a break to open the day's mail. There was a letter from our home owners' insurance company, so I expected an update on the best new flood insurance product or a reminder about possible discounts if a customer would pay semi-annually; so, I opened it with interest. To my surprise, I saw the enticing headline: "Guaranteed Income for life could be missing from your retirement plan." The following paragraph featured the words in bold print, **"steady stream of income."** Then there was the grim reminder that "only 21% of Americans are confident that they have saved enough for retirement." And, finally, the good news/bad news about longevity risk, that "there is a 72% chance that if you or your spouse reach age 65 that you will live to age 85." Restated, your money will have to last you a long time, so a guaranteed income stream for life is very important for you.

This was obviously a promotion for tax-deferred annuities. Moments later there was an ad on television reminding me that there was a strong possibility this current, over-valued market would crash and, therefore, the salesperson—a well-known actor—was buying gold...or silver or platinum...or all three. He concluded by saying, "you cannot really call something an investment unless you can hold it in your hand, can you?" Later in the day another "trusted" TV personality was telling me that reverse mortgages really do make sense. The next day on my way to the store, I tuned into the local radio station that was announcing its lineup of shows for the day:

- ~ 9 am–The Financial Connection
- ~ 10 am–The Financial Game Plan
- ~ 11 am–The [Financial Planner's name] Weekly Show
- ~ 1 pm–Wall Street Update with…

Each of these radio/commercials provided opportunities for a retiree or soon to be retiree to get more information about the financial landscape and advice on what to do to be successful in retirement. There are so many opinions, and I listen to many of them if I happen to be in the car, trusting…well, maybe, hoping that there may be a gem in all of this somewhere. Maybe I can hear about an approach that makes sense in a special or a certain situation. I dismiss nothing, but I take everything with a grain of salt and a healthy dose of skepticism. Believe me there is no absence of information to sift through; but remember that the "teasers" they use—like asking you to read their Financial Heart Attack newsletter about the impending Market crash—are chosen to play on your fear of losing your hard-earned assets. They may be doing you a service by reminding you that stock market volatility is a threat, but we all know that fear is at best only a short-term motivator.

⚷ Key Reminders

~ Remember that risk and volatility are not the same.

~ The variety of types of risks associated with investing are important to know about but not something you need to be an expert in.

~ Paying attention to interest rates and inflation is important to all retirees.

~ Always understand what fees and taxes can do to erode your cash flow.

~ Understand that how long you live and how high inflation is are important variables in your investment decisions.

~ Don't believe everything you receive in the mail or hear on radio or the television or read on the internet. Take everything with a grain of salt; study the concepts; and then ask the pertinent questions.

11

MANAGE WHAT YOU CAN CONTROL

---

*"Sometimes the poorest person leaves
the richest inheritance."*
—Ruth E. Renkel

There are a variety of quotes I have collected that are used to help retirees (and others) recall important truisms in life. A number of them seem aimed at the retiree market and are worth repeating as we begin this section of the book on wills and trusts, i.e. estate planning:

"Planning is a process of choosing among those many options. If we do not choose to plan, then we chose to have others plan for us."

"You can't take it with you."

"He or she who has the most gold (or toys) wins at the end."

"You can't control what happens to your money after you die."

"Some families trying to work their way through inheritance issues can become the most dysfunctional groups imaginable." (Actually, books have been written on this subject that present the best way to go about educating families about and protecting families from this insanity and depravity.)

Another group we work with likened the process to a jigsaw puzzle for which there are many pieces that need to be put in proper order to make sense and provide you satisfaction at the end of the process.

Assuming that all of this is true, what can you do to take a modicum of control to ensure that the process of having your possessions, after death, go to those you actually would want to have receive them? And further to ensure that all this will happen in a timely and economical way.

Unfortunately, there is a persuasive myth that if you do not have much in the way of resources, you do not need to do any estate planning. Furthermore, some assume you do not even need a will unless you have a great deal to bequeath to others. These are clearly myths that need to be debunked. There are far too many people in the process of preparing for retirement who are unaware of the risks they face if they do nothing to protect their interests and to memorialize their wishes through formal documentation.

A basic premise for inheritance planning should be to protect your assets, regardless how bountiful or how limited they are, by creating at least a will to direct those you leave behind in how to disperse your belongings. At a minimum everyone who has a family now, everyone still working, and everyone now in retirement needs to have at least a basic will.

A will provides basic coverage for all your interests, including your dependents and personal possessions. Even the most rudimentary will qualifies as a legal instrument and gives you legal protections for the delivery of your possessions after your death according to your stated wishes. For that matter, even having your intentions written out on a napkin or yellow theme pad may be better than nothing, though even rudimentary written instructions must take into consideration your State's requirements and statutes in order to be considered valid. While that may have been considered an onerous burden years ago, with will writing services as available on-line as they are today, getting a simple will that is legal is both easy and inexpensive. Bottom line: there is no excuse for not having a will and every reason to have one. Consider it another best practice for you. And in a perfect world, you would take the additional step of having an attorney at least read it over to ensure you have met the applicable State statutes.

Imagine the repercussions of not having one. In the worst possible scenario, no one will know who is responsible for raising your children or dependents. Is that a decision you want to leave to your State's agencies? Would you ever want there to be a lack of clarity about your custody plan for your children or your dependents? A will provides the necessary and important clarity. Then there are your belongings. To whom does the house go? What about those special collections? Who inherits the IRA or 401(k)? Who gets the car? What happens to your debts? Whose responsibility is settling debts, and what resources should be used? Without a will, you give away control of truly important decisions about your possessions and your dependents. Imagine these decisions being left to others by default?

Support for Estate Planning

Since most people understand why a will is important, we can move on to second order decision-making: Should you engage estate attorneys or not? Should you consider creating trusts, or not bother with nor assume the cost of creating trusts? Should you create revocable trusts or irrevocable trusts? Questions, questions, questions. And they are all important ones. Unfortunately, and as you would imagine, there are no easy answers to these questions. Estate attorneys can be expensive, depending on what you want them to do. They can, however, also be reasonable if you do the leg work and simply ask your attorney to review your process and work product. It may also be possible to arrange a fair price determined by the level of complexity of the estate. Remember, an estate does not automatically connote millions of dollars or complex structures. Your estate is simply what you own and you want to have a say about in its distribution.

Trusts

Things have changed dramatically when it comes to trusts. Years ago, only the very wealthy individuals or families took the time, expense, or trouble or had the need to establish trusts. More recently, however, people with straight forward estates have determined that paying to set up a trust is worthwhile to help one avoid specific complications after one's death. There are numerous reasons for this change in thinking:

- ~ Trusts make it easier to ensure that your assets will pass to your designated beneficiary/ies without certain taxes or costs.
- ~ Trusts will guarantee that the details of one's estate remain private rather than matters of public record.
- ~ Trusts will allow you to avoid the potentially time-consuming probate process.

All these are good reasons to consider the cost/benefit of paying to have a trust or several trusts created. Trusts are simply estate management vehicles. They may not be for everyone but may work perfectly for many others. They are also not perfect and do not solve all the issues relating to estate planning, but they are helpful in creating the control we discussed earlier in this chapter.

As importantly, however, trusts are certainly not strategies you should be talked into. As with almost all else we have discussed in this primer, before you buy or commit to any product or process, make certain you know what you are getting into. As with investing, you should never participate in or purchase something you do not understand; and you should not deal with those who want to sell you something you do not need or cannot afford.

Revocable Trusts or Revocable Living Trusts

Revocable trusts or living trusts are, as their names indicate, trusts that can be revoked or changed by those setting them up. When you set up a revocable trust, you are stating your intentions for how the assets in your trust will be distributed or used after your death. However, and this is important, you are not committing your assets irretrievably to this plan. You are setting your plan in motion by memorializing your intentions in case something happens to you before you expect it to happen or if your circumstances were to change. You are also benefiting from the protection of probate at the time of your passing. Once the estate documents have been created and signed and the trusts established, there is a secondary step: funding the trust with the assets that you want to protect from probate and want to pass on to your heirs with as much privacy and as little delay as is possible. You are not required to fund the trusts, but if you do not and were to pass away with the trusts unfunded, the trusts would be null and void and you would have missed the opportunity to protect them. Then there is a third step you can take but do not need to take which is to set these Trusts in place forever by making them irrevocable, meaning unable to be changed by the grantor…you. Revocable trusts retain flexibility during your lifetime, and while this does not provide you with tax protection during your lifetime as your trust assets grow, these trusts will become automatically irrevocable upon your death, thereby shielding them from probate and its costs, time delays, and lack of privacy.

Irrevocable Trusts

The other approach is to create irrevocable trusts which lock you in to your estate plan forever (or as close to forever as there can be) and in exchange for the certitude of the commitment of your estate plan, provides you with certain protections throughout your lifetime. Generally speaking, irrevocable trusts are set up when a grantor (you) knows exactly where his or her or their assets will go at the time of death. Their irrevocable trusts are fully funded with their assets, and that funding, along with the commitment to agree to the terms of the estate documents, relieve them of certain burdens during their lifetime because the assets are legally no longer theirs. The terms of these trusts can no longer be changed by those who set them up, but since the trust assets are no longer theirs, they can be protected during their lives from taxes on these assets or the responsibility of having a high net worth when it comes to assessing their ability to pay for things like nursing home care. (Note: The questions surrounding a person's ability to pay for nursing home care when there are resources in an irrevocable trust will lead anyone in that situation to regulations and requirements relating to look back periods and the laws governing this specific area of elder care and law. For example, setting up an irrevocable trust immediately before enrolling in a nursing home to avoid the obligation of paying for the care is not permissible. Forward thinking and planning is required.)

Other Trusts

This is not the place to go into greater detail about the variety of trusts that can be helpful and/or important in estate planning. There are a number of charitable trusts, life income trusts, property trusts, insurance trusts, and generation-skipping trusts. All of these can be the right instrument for the right person depending on the circumstances. Suffice it to say for this aspect of retirement planning that educating yourself about the general explanations of their uses and values before you talk to an attorney makes the most sense. And the internet or readily available books online can serve as your guides. Then, it is wise to consider carefully how helpful or appropriate the decision might be for you before signing up for the cost of creating such a document. Things do not have to be complicated to be helpful. Remember that grain of salt, and always measure twice before you cut once.

Our Journey with Wills and Trusts

Pam and I began our estate planning process more than 40 years ago in the office of a young lawyer when we decided to have basic wills drawn up, primarily because we wanted the guardians of our children, if we lost our lives unexpectedly, to have clear direction on how we wanted them to carry on in our absence. Nearly twenty years later, just after we had moved to a new state, we made an appointment with an estate attorney (who came highly recommended) to update our basic, individual wills (we each have always had a separate, personal will) with a more experienced estate attorney. By this time our children were grown with families of their own, and we wanted to reflect the changes in their and our lives in our new wills. We also needed to ensure that our wills reflected the requirements and statutes of our new state. Powers of Attorney and health care directives were different in our new home state, and we needed to update and change the language in them. We did not set up trusts at that time, but our estate attorney helped us understand the concept of trusts and how they might support or strengthen our planning.

We met with this new attorney every few years—a good approach to follow—in order to keep our wills up to date, but then he retired. We were also nearing retirement, but we felt the need to have our estate documents in place before we actually entered retirement, so we engaged another estate attorney to discuss the benefits and costs of creating estate planning documents that included trusts. We had more moving parts in our personal situation at this juncture, so we selected a person who could help us develop what we expected would be the final plan. The expense was not unreasonable, and the service would, we were convinced, simplify our estate process.

Although we believed we had completed the last step in planning our estate, when we retired officially and moved to a new state, we realized that the statutes of the new state had to be incorporated into our estate documents. We interviewed a number of estate attorneys in the area and engaged a wonderful professional to ensure that we had dotted all the i's and crossed all the t's. We were surprised by what had to be done to make our wills and trusts compliant with our new state's statutes. Once again, we needed different language for the living will documents, in the financial and health care Powers of Attorney documents, and even for our revocable living trusts.

We agreed with our attorney that we would make an appointment with her regularly to determine if there were changes in our planning or in our situations that merited changes in the plan. Clearly, we believed the cost of getting these documents right was worth the peace of mind we desired as we contemplated this important chapter of our life process. Now, we believed we were fully ready for the future.

As a reference for you, our estate plan included a living trust for each of us which we decided to fund immediately with physical assets including our home and non-retirement, taxable savings. (Note: One cannot include qualified, tax-deferred assets in a trust since taxes have not yet been paid on them.) We did not choose to create an irrevocable trust since we were not looking for the tax protections afforded by that strategy at that time. And we are each the beneficiaries of one another's trust.

Important Conversations and Communications

Before I move on from this topic, I think it might be helpful to describe some of the more personal parts of the process, which involved the conversations that Pam and I had as we discussed the goals we had agreed should and would guide our estate planning process. As I pointed out earlier in this primer, almost every process ought to begin with a statement of goals and objectives as well as our value proposition—that sometimes elusive fourth pillar of retirement I mentioned in Chapter Two. Couples need to create a respectful and responsible process to determine what the important questions are and what values will help guide you to answer them. What are the outcomes you are seeking? What legacy will that plan represent for your family? How and when—timing—should you communicate all of this to your family? What lessons will you be teaching your children and grandchildren by how you handle this opportunity/responsibility? Will you walk the talk in your decision-making?

There was a lot to consider, and we wanted to do this planning well. Most importantly, we wanted to do it together, so the plan truly represented our thinking.

Then there are the important questions about the reality of what your assets will be worth at the time of your death. What will you have at the end of your life? Who, if anyone, will still be depending on you for financial support? How will you ensure that needed support is fully arranged and carried out? What strategies and products will you use to ensure success in the planning?

Once these decisions had been made, or at least mostly formed, then we needed to plan the conversations we wanted to have with our children and other beneficiaries; and we realized these conversations are not always without their challenges. Talking about end of life issues can be difficult and emotional. Talking about money is hard to do as well. There may be expectations about what will be forthcoming for each beneficiary; there may also be the difficulties of changing one's perspective when the conversation has changed from something that seemed a long way off to a reality with a timeline—a prospect which can make these conversations highly charged and emotional.

One well-to-do person in the news reportedly said that he had changed his estate plan recently because he couldn't bear the thought that his children might be sitting around waiting for him and/or his wife to pass away so they could receive their inheritance. He also said he didn't just want his wife and him to be viewed as the wealthy grandparents who gave the best and most expensive gifts. He had calculated that he and his wife had plenty to live on and that they would enjoy seeing their children and grandchildren and the charities they had decided to support enjoy their inheritances while they were alive. "If we wait until we are dead," he mused, "we won't get to see how much good we were able to do."

The other challenge for us and for other retirees, I imagine, was not getting consumed by the constant pressure to increase our holdings for the benefit of our heirs. You can miss all the fun you had saved your entire career to be able to have, by focusing on building increasingly more assets to leave to your beneficiaries. Remember, you spent a life time creating more value—in your home, bank account, investment profile, or other tangible assets— so your final years could be relaxing and fun. Doing this created habits in saving and goal-setting, so it only makes sense that you would want to continue to build or acquire. It may be surprisingly challenging to change your focus to simply enjoying the fruits of your labor. There sometimes is a psychological barrier to spending what has been created by habitual savings behaviors that can be powerful and hard to get over—literally and figuratively. So, you need to go back to the answers to the what questions and the value proposition you agreed upon when you planned your retirement. Remember: *Make the plan; work the plan!*

For all these reasons goal setting and values clarification are essential. Let's say for a moment that philanthropy is important to you. In our case, Pam and I have always made a habit of supporting organizations and institutions in which we believe and which we have planned to benefit through our estate planning. Our thinking had been that our favorite charities would be a part of our legacy. We certainly do not have a level of asset accumulation that could transform a major charity, but as we have always practiced through our giving, we have wanted to at least do our fair share. We also have modeled this value and the behavior that accompanies it for our children and grandchildren. We hope and believe the value of supporting and serving others has become a part of their experience and their value system; and this will mean that any decision we make with our resources to benefit charities will be welcomed and understood by them. While we believe it will, we are also trying to determine whether it would be more appropriate to set up our trusts so our beneficiaries have the flexibility to support their own special causes with what will then be their money. Maybe setting up a small charity fund which they can manage, makes the most sense. We will decide that only after receiving their input and making sure it makes sense for Pam and me.

I am confident we will get to the right decision, and I expect it will be a thoughtful and reasoned one. We do not plan on leaving something so important to chance. We will have asked ourselves the right questions throughout our journey in order to do the right things.

As I conclude this chapter, I want to share the best new recommendation I have heard about recently in estate planning. The concept is including in your estate documents a final letter. Pam and I joke that is the modern version of the, "If you are reading this letter, it means…." that you read about or see in murder mysteries or old movies and westerns. The letter, however, is your last chance to make your wishes and value proposition known; to pass on the names and addresses of the important members of your team—estate attorney or lawyer, accountant, insurance agent, and financial person or people; and to express your personal feelings to those inheriting what you have left behind, such as why we left this to you and what motivated us to save this for you. As such it is a combination of statements of the heart and the head, the practical and the emotional.

We are planning on creating such a letter now and sharing it long before our deaths with our children and grandchildren as another lesson in the importance of good planning. Maybe this will be one more teachable moment in their preparation for creating their own legacies in the future. Furthermore, we expect it to be a nice and more gentle way to have the conversation about what is the inevitable last act for all of us.

This chapter's best practice would have to be to understand that however large or small your estate, it represents your legacy and it is important to you and to others. What you do with your possessions at the time of your death is a personal decision, but it is also intensely important for those who survive you, not only children and grandchildren, but also for those who follow them. What you planned for, which you believed were realistic and aspirational goals, matter—now and in the future. You want to get this right.

O─ Key Reminders

~ "Sometimes the poorest people leave the richest inheritances."—Ruth E. Renkel

~ Never imagine that what you will leave behind for your heirs or assigns is not worth the effort of planning your estate with a will or a trust.

~ Trusts can provide numerous guarantees relating to lower taxes, the avoidance of probate, and privacy.

~ Planning is meant to be shared with heirs and assigns, and it is helpful to have those important conversations in an honest and timely manner.

~ Remember that the value proposition is best served when you work the plan that you made, and you make the plan that will serve your true needs and values best.

~ If real estate decision-making is about location, location, location, so is estate planning. Where you reside and where you die matter because different states have different statutes for estate planning as well as different laws relating to people who die while in their states.

~ Make certain you leave a letter of intent as part of your estate documents.

12

PLANNING ENSURES A BETTER FUTURE

*"Planning is the bringing of the future
into the present so that you can do
something about it now."*
—Anon

As Pam and I evaluate whether we made our way successfully
into and through the retiring process, we realize there were
many things we did right but so many we never believed would
be important. Fortunately, we managed to get the big ones mostly
right. We saved in a disciplined way and always made certain we
paid ourselves first (putting money into our savings accounts and
investments). We understood the importance of wills and estate
planning early on. We had parents who taught us the value of
education. I remember vividly my father explaining to me early on
in my life that he had spent his resources up front ensuring that
all eight of his children would receive a first-rate education: my
inheritance was my education.

Pam's parents were equally committed to ensuring that their
grandchildren would be able to afford an excellent education and

introduced us to the concept of generation-skipping vehicles for education before it was in vogue. We joke that we may have had one of the first 529 college savings plans in the nation. That was a part of their legacy, and today two of our seven grandchildren have already benefited from both his generosity and his example. We were part of legacies that helped us formulate positive value systems. Our families also helped us understand the differences between the nice-to-have and the essential-to-have. They both had many choices to make in life, but they helped us to learn how to make these important decisions among so many options.

There is an important, if apocryphal, story about a university professor who was making a point to his class about determining what was important in intellectual inquiry. He asked a student to come forward to help him make his point. He pulled out a large trash can and asked the student to fill it up with large stones in the front of the room. When the student had filled the can to the brim, the professor asked him, "Is the can full now?"

The student looked down and responded, "It certainly is."

"But," said the professor, "what if I were to ask you to add in all of these smaller stones in the cracks and crevices? Could you fit more into the barrel?"

The student thought for a moment, nodded, and proceeded to fill in the open spaces in the barrel with the smaller rocks.

Then the professor asked again: "So, is it now full?"

"Yes, it is," replied the student confidently.

"But what if I were to ask you to add all this gravel in a pile off stage to the barrel? Would the gravel fit in as well?" queried the professor.

"I guess so," the student responded with a smile as he added the smaller pieces of gravel.

"Well, then I guess it is finally full. Would you agree?" the professor asked once again.

"I think it must be, but I imagine it is not," added the student in response.

"Correct," said the professor, "because we still have water which I have no doubt will also fit in."

So, what's the moral of the story? If you want to do the complete job, whether in matters human, intellectual, or physical, begin with the big rocks. There are so many details that can bog you down, even paralyze you. These smaller matters tend to take up a great deal of space and often lead to your not having the room or the time to do the truly important work in front of you. Therefore, once you have attended to getting the big rocks in place, then you can address the smaller issues and those small details that are important to include.

This is a favorite reminder I have cited often when working with teams on projects and problems. Let's put what really matters on the table, or in the conversation, first. Only by dealing with the big, important questions first will you ultimately address the overarching question or problem in its entirety.

I think of this scenario when addressing the question of retirement planning. Retirement is filled with little technical problems, just like those I encountered with my technology glitches, Medicare sign-up, and insurances. Yes, not knowing what I needed to, cost me some valuable time. Maybe securing the safety of my initial document in that process was a big rock. I guess I imagined that all that counted was getting the word on the page. In reality, getting this information to people who would benefit from it was really the big rock.

A secondary lesson may have been that while you cannot accomplish as much if you fail to put the big rocks in first, you still need the smaller stones, the gravel, and the water to make the most of the experience. Knowing about backing up my documents and not hitting the keys as emphatically might have made this exercise less painful; but I am not certain it would have made it better. I was able to re-route and determine what I now knew to be the big rocks. I wanted to smooth out the glide path into retirement for others who would follow Pam and me. I thought our story would be interesting because of the unusual circumstances we were coming from, but I have realized everyone's and every couple's retirements are special and different.

What is not different are the ways of thinking about and making sense of the retirement challenges. Therefore, I will end with my big seven for retirement planning and for life in general. These reminders have served us well for nearly four decades of administrative responsibility and organizational leadership and more recently in retirement:

- Life is a cost/benefit analysis.
- Make the plan; then work the plan. Leadership always requires action.
- "Culture eats strategy for breakfast every time."—Peter Drucker
- Timing is everything.
- "Doing the job right is not as important as doing the right job."—General Ulmer
- Put the big rocks in first.
- "Seek not the simplicity on this side of complexity; seek the simplicity on the other side of complexity."—Oliver Wendell Holmes

What I cannot tell you is how to invest. I can only tell you that you need to save and invest. I cannot tell you whether to put your 401(k) or 403(b) dollars into fixed income vehicles, equity funds, or balanced accounts. I can tell you to take full advantage of the tax deferral guaranteed by retirement programs. I cannot tell you whether or not you should be thoughtful and careful about over-funding your tax deferred plans. I can tell you that you need to ask the question and do the analysis of a tax-deferral at all costs strategy. Whether you need funding for those with individual financial needs after your death is not an analysis I can make. I can tell you that there is no one-size-fits-all approach. There are, however, big rocks and rules of thumb that I can point to as critically important when planning for retirement. There are also certain behaviors that will lead to positive outcomes, and there is homework that needs to be done.

As important, all this planning and preparation is not easy to do alone. Your role is to frame and then answer the questions. How to enact the strategy probably will require the support of professionals. And I do not mean the "professionals" on the radio. Now, I have never actually spoken to one of the radio financial pros, but at the very least, having personal interviews with those you are considering using and doing reference checking on them would represent the minimum you should do before choosing financial planners, estate attorneys or lawyers, insurance companies and agents, and accountants. These can be important members of your team, and you need to be able to trust them, understand them, and afford them. Trust is the basis of all positive relationships. Understanding a person's motivation, values, and message is essential. Too many people planning their retirements rue the day they purchased products they did not understand from people they did not really know and trust.

And, finally, you always need to understand the cost of the approaches being sold to you. Fees, commissions, premiums, and tax ramifications matter; they can erode hard-earned profit or income if not managed properly and understood. Remember that even as we speak or write, the rules and agreements that apply to retirement are changing. The ground on taxes, health care, welfare programs, and federal benefits and write-offs is shifting under our feet. For instance, how do we know that tax-free bonds will always be tax-free? This issue was one of the discussion points in the new Tax Cut and Jobs Act (TCJA). If tax free bonds had lost their tax advantaged status, and if a person had bet heavily on the tax-free nature of these vehicles for their retirement funding, they might have been faced with having to do additional planning, finding a new approach to realizing their goals, and then assessing the success of the new approach. Staying fluid is critically important in this process.

My primer was written as a way of introducing people to a way of thinking, to a process-centered approach to planning, and to a "questions first" discipline. Nothing here is rocket science. It is mostly common sense. I hope it helps you plan and enjoy your retirement. And I hope you will think of Pam and me continuing the process that we are enjoying so much in spite of all of the surprises we had. Putting the big rocks in first proved to be extremely important, and answering the right questions led to ensuring the right actions. We remind ourselves often that life is a series of cost/benefit analyses. Life decisions are made more thoughtfully when one remembers that timing is a key variable. And, finally, while you are working your plan, you must have as your north star your value proposition—it will guide you. Enjoy!

Index